wrote about in her first book, *Change of Heart*. This time Jeanne revisits her hometown—Oklahoma City—to tell the unforgettable story of a meeting between Bud Welsh, whose daughter, Julie, was killed in the Oklahoma City bombing, and Bill McVeigh, whose son, Timothy, detonated the truck bomb that killed Julie, killed one hundred sixty-seven other innocents, and wounded hundreds more. This meeting was an act of grace which transformed both men and helped lift them up and out from under the rubble of their lives after the bombing. And this book—also an act of grace—is bound to elevate and transform all who read it.

—Steve Drizin and Laura Nirider, CODIRECTORS,
CENTER ON WRONGFUL CONVICTIONS

Jeanne Bishop has written such a moving book, about an unexpected friendship between two men, a relationship whose foundation is the capacity to forgive. *Grace from the Rubble* reminds us that sometimes we can find the best of who we are in the worst of times.

—Alex Kotlowitz, BESTSELLING AUTHOR, *THERE ARE NO CHILDREN HERE* AND *AN AMERICAN SUMMER*

In *Grace from the Rubble* Jeanne Bishop provides us with a genuine testament that compassion and empathy are the most powerful and only weapons against hate.

—Christian Picciolini, AUTHOR, *BREAKING HATE: CONFRONTING THE NEW CULTURE OF EXTREMISM*

Jeanne Bishop's unflinching, strong voice is one we need to hear in our divided nation. She is no naive bleeding heart; rather she is in her third decade as a public defender brave enough to regularly walk into Chicago jails and meet alone with those convicted of violent crimes. She is a bold, gritty storyteller, and Bud and Bill are a compelling story. For those who seek more love in the world and a path beyond our divisions, Bishop shows the way.

—Prof. Mark Osler, ROBERT AND MARION SHORT
DISTINGUISHED CHAIR, UNIVERSITY OF ST. THOMAS

GRACE
from the
RUBBLE

GRACE
from the
RUBBLE

TWO FATHERS' ROAD TO RECONCILIATION

AFTER THE OKLAHOMA CITY BOMBING

JEANNE BISHOP

ZONDERVAN BOOKS

ZONDERVAN BOOKS

Grace from the Rubble
Copyright © 2020 by Jeanne Bishop

Requests for information should be addressed to:
Zondervan, *3900 Sparks Dr. SE, Grand Rapids, Michigan 49546*

Zondervan titles may be purchased in bulk for educational, business, fundraising, or sales promotional use. For information, please email SpecialMarkets@Zondervan.com.

ISBN 978-0-310-35769-8 (audio)

Library of Congress Cataloging-in-Publication Data
Names: Bishop, Jeanne, author.
Title: Grace from the rubble : two fathers' road to reconciliation after the Oklahoma City bombing / Jeanne Bishop.
Description: Grand Rapids : Zondervan, 2020. | Summary: "Grace from the Rubble by Jeanne Bishop tells the riveting true story of how tragedy destined two men to become enemies - the father of a daughter killed in the Oklahoma City bombing and the father of her killer - and the astonishing journey that led them to forge an extraordinary friendship"—Provided by publisher.
Identifiers: LCCN 2019050070 (print) | LCCN 2019050071 (ebook) | ISBN 9780310357674 (hardcover) | ISBN 9780310357681 (ebook)
Subjects: LCSH: Forgiveness—Religious aspects—Christianity. | Oklahoma City Federal Building Bombing, Oklahoma City, Okla., 1995. | Violence—Religious aspects—Christianity.
Classification: LCC BV4647.F55 B574 2020 (print) | LCC BV4647.F55 (ebook) | DDC 976.6/38053—dc23
LC record available at https://lccn.loc.gov/2019050070
LC ebook record available at https://lccn.loc.gov/2019050071

Published in association with the literary agency of Daniel Literary Group, LLC, Brentwood, TN.

"A Casady Hymn," quoted in chapter 1, appears courtesy of Casady School. Music by H. P. Gersman, lyrics by E. Sloan. Special thanks to Father Tim Sean Youmans, Vicar of St. Edward the Confessor Chapel and Religious Life Department Chair, Casady School.

The words from the panel in the Oklahoma City National Memorial and Museum quoted in chapter 4, and from the Survivor Tree promontory quoted in chapter 8, are courtesy of the museum. Thank you to Helen Stiefmiller, Collections Manager.

Several quotes in chapter 6 appear with permission from the book displayed for Julie Marie Welch in the Oklahoma City National Memorial and Museum: *Their Faith Has Touched Us: The Legacies of Three Young Oklahoma City Bombing Victims* by Maria Ruiz Scaperlanda (Sheed and Ward, 1998). Thank you to Patricia Zline, Rights and Permissions Assistant, Rowman and Littlefield.

Quotes from the poems of Carol Hamilton, "Braced Against the Wind" from an anthology by the same name, and "Face of War" from *Shots On* (Finishing Line Press) are used with gracious permission of the author.

The quote from the official record of the Oklahoma City bombing in chapter 7 is used with permission of *Oklahoma Today* magazine. Thank you to Colleen McIntyre, Director of Operations.

Quotes of Jan Henry, Chris Fields, and Florence Rogers in chapter 7 are from the play *In the Middle of the West* by Steve Gilroy, with kind permission of the author.

Cover design: Studio Gearbox
Cover photos: Pics-xl / SasaStock / Shutterstock
Author photo: Scott Friesen
Interior design: Denise Froehlich

Printed in the United States of America

20 21 22 23 LSC 10 9 8 7 6 5 4 3 2 1

DEDICATION

*For my father, M. Lee Bishop, and
my sons, Brendan and Stephen*

Que bien sé yo la fuente que mana y corre,
Aunque es de noche.

———

For I know well the spring that flows and runs,
Although it is night.

—ST. JOHN OF THE CROSS

* These words are inscribed on a piece of granite from the Alfred P. Murrah Federal Building in Oklahoma City and dedicated to Julie Marie Welch, near a fountain outside her church.

CONTENTS

PREFACE

Once, there were three families: Bud's, Bill's, and mine. Each family had three children. Mine included my two sisters and me; we grew up in Oklahoma City, a place as sturdy as the red clay of its soil and as open as its wide horizons. Bud Welch, a gas station owner from Oklahoma City, had three children, two boys and one girl. Bill McVeigh, an auto parts worker from faraway western New York, had two daughters and one son.

Bud, Bill, and I are linked by tragedy; each of us lost one of our family members to a deliberate killing. All of them died young.

I lost my younger sister, Nancy, in April 1990. A teenaged boy broke into her home on Chicago's North Shore and shot her and her husband to death. When Nancy died at twenty-five, the child she was carrying in her womb, my first little niece or nephew, died with her.

Five years later to the month, Bud Welch's only daughter, Julie, age twenty-three, perished in the Oklahoma City bombing. A truck full of explosives destroyed the federal building where she worked and took the lives of 168 people, including hers.

The last to die was the man who, at the age of twenty-six, set off that bomb on the streets of Oklahoma City: Timothy McVeigh. The federal government executed him for his crime six years later. His father, Bill McVeigh, despite his pleas to spare his child, lost his only son.

The nexus linking Bud, Bill, and me is Oklahoma City, a place broken but unbowed by evil. Oklahoma City lost its children too. Evil was not the end of the story, though. It never is.

Love did not leave me in the place I was when Nancy and her husband and their baby were buried in the earth. Love led me out of that deep valley to a mailbox where I stood with a letter in hand, addressed to the prison where the young man who killed Nancy was serving a life sentence, telling him that I had forgiven him and reaching out to reconcile. It was in the course of that trek from fear to freedom that I found Bud, and then Bill, two men who showed me what heartbreak and courage and love look like, my heroes of reconciliation.

We sometimes imagine that it is facts and argument that change us, but as a lawyer I know that isn't true. Few people are transformed by argument. Everyone, though, has been transformed by a story—our lived experience or the narrative of a life around us. Those linger long after the telling is done. All of us long for stories that transport us, that dispel our fears, that inspire and illumine, stories that will live on in the heart.

I know such a story. It is a true one of a place in the heartland and the tragedy that struck there, and of the two good men, two fathers, who found each other in the tangled aftermath.

Vengeance begets vengeance; hate breeds more hate. Reconciliation is altogether different; it changes us and changes the world, one human heart at a time.

These two fathers, Bud and Bill, the father of a daughter slain and the father of her slayer, should have been enemies; earthly reason would have dictated so. But that is not what happened.

PART 1 | The Characters

CHAPTER 1

OKLAHOMA CITY

Cataclysms are the story.
Our cities sprang up overnight,
Are flattened at a tongue-lashing
By clouds and bush-whackers, and
Bonnies and Clydes
Struck fast and hid against
The land stretched and pegged
Flat to the Four Corners
Of the Earth. We do not cower
At disaster.

—CAROL HAMILTON, poet laureate
of Oklahoma at the time of the
Oklahoma City bombing in 1995,
from "Braced Against the Wind"

The story begins in Oklahoma City, a place of tornados and fractured earth.

I grew up there in a brick house at 6609 Hillcrest Avenue. My family moved to Oklahoma City the year I had just turned ten. My younger sister, Nancy, was five and my older sister, Jennifer, was twelve. My father, Lee Bishop, was a lawyer working as general counsel to a meatpacking company that had opened a new headquarters there. My mother, Joyce Bishop, worked full time raising us girls and part time performing the music and theater she loved.

We'd come to Oklahoma City, after a brief stint in Dallas, from a lakefront suburb on Chicago's North Shore. The cool, green village of Winnetka, Illinois, was as different from Oklahoma City as pebbles in frigid Lake Michigan water are from Oklahoma's sunbaked soil.

The leaves in the tall trees outside our Winnetka house made a sound like rain when the wind tossed. On winter nights, frost on my bedroom window sparkled in the glow from the streetlight outside. I would walk to school in snow boots and pants, knee-deep in soft white powder, shielding my small face from sleet with my scarf.

My mother and I would ride the Metra train into the city, with its tall silver canyons of skyscrapers; solid, graceful bridges spanning the Chicago River; and elegant women laden with shopping bags strolling down Michigan Avenue.

When my parents told us we were moving to Texas, then Oklahoma, I imagined small, dusty towns with

bar doors swinging in the wind and tumbleweeds roll-
ing down the street past a cow skull. My Western-movie
images of the place were, of course, wildly wrong.

Oklahoma City was an expansive metropolis sprawling over five counties, with green neighborhoods nestled
between stretches of highway, and downtown buildings
spread out rather than clustered like Chicago's. The
city had deliberately expanded, incorporating suburban
areas like mine until it became the largest city, landwise,
in the world.

The city had grown up in fitful spurts and waves.
After President Andrew Jackson signed the Indian
Removal Act in 1830, the US government forcibly
moved indigenous men, women, and children from
their homes on the Eastern Seaboard to territory in what
would become Oklahoma. Next, after the Civil War,
came ranchers and cowboys to herd cattle coming from
Texas across Oklahoma to the railroads in Kansas.

Then came the land runs in 1889. The federal
government divided what was once "Indian Territory"
into two parts, one for Native Americans and one for
mostly white settlers. Would-be landowners were promised one hundred sixty acres of land if the settlers agreed
to live on it for at least five years. The US Army shot off
a cannon on April 22 to announce the start of the run.
A throng of one hundred thousand people poured in, on
mule or horseback, in wagons and on foot, to claim the
land. By the next day, Oklahoma City was a tent city of
ten thousand people.

Another wave followed not long after, spurred by a new industry: oil. After the first commercial oil wells appeared in the late 1800s, people hoping to strike it rich flocked to Oklahoma City, nearly doubling the population. The discovery in 1928 of a huge reservoir of oil—the second largest in the world—drew even more people to the city's booming economy just as the nation's was about to crash.

The summer we moved in, the air was an oven blast of warmth with no hint of the cool that tinged Chicago's summer evenings. The light in Oklahoma City was brighter, turned up a notch, as if a knob on our old TV set had been dialed from muted darkness to pale brightness. The horizon, uncluttered by trees or skyscrapers, stretched wider and farther than my eyes had ever seen.

The summer lawns in front of the houses in Nichols Hills, our new neighborhood, were not plush and emerald colored like those in Winnetka; the grass was hard and brown, baked from the sun to a crispy texture. Some people painted their lawns with a fertilizer that turned them a loud tennis-court green.

Oklahoma dirt was red from the iron oxide in it. When the wind lifted the dirt and blew it around, the air turned a burnt-orange hue. The next morning, the gray streets and sidewalks were like pastries decorated with swirls of reddish-brown icing, a glaze of dust and dew.

Trees valiantly grew in an ongoing struggle with sun and wind and one other foe: mistletoe. Everywhere, the trees were clogged with it. I loved learning that mistletoe was the Oklahoma state plant—a symbol of Christmas in this warm place! Waxy green clusters grew in the branches and spread till people knocked them down with rakes.

Sidewalks were almost nonexistent in my neighborhood and the ones nearby. Cars ruled. Once, years later, when I was walking a few blocks from the store carrying a bag of groceries in each hand, drivers slowed down to stare; one woman rolled down her car window and called out, "Do you need help, hon?"

My father drove us around the "city" part of Oklahoma City to see his new office. The sand-colored, spacious downtown was more sparse than the crowded streets of Chicago. I learned later that people were underground, in a network of tunnels filled with walkways, shops, and restaurants that shielded pedestrians from the grainy wind.

We got to see the stockyards of Cowtown, once the largest cattle market in the world. Cattle and hogs came in from states stretching from Iowa to New Mexico to be auctioned off in Oklahoma City. Flanking the livestock pens were restaurants like the Cattlemen's Steakhouse, where I ate a breakfast of chicken-fried steak, biscuits, and cream gravy. Nearby shops sold real leather cowboy boots and long-sleeved shirts with pearl snaps.

The state capitol building was most striking of all, with a working oil well on its lawn. This one was tall and latticed; other oil rigs we saw around the city looked like praying mantises, huge steel insects bending down, then up, then down again, dipping their noses to the ground.

Our house faced west, looking over rooftops to a golf course just beyond. On our second floor, two leaded windows opened over a circle driveway in front. When I was older, my little sister, Nancy, would spy on me from those windows. She would lift the latches that held the windows tightly in place, turn the small metal cranks that rolled the windows open, and peer down, calling out, "Hey! What are you doing?" just as some boy I liked was lingering at the front door saying good night.

My sisters and I desperately wanted to see a tornado from those windows. We watched for signs of one whenever it stormed. The sky would turn muddy gray and morph into a spectral green, the color of the face of the Wicked Witch of the West in *The Wizard of Oz*. Clouds would roil and churn. Flocks of blackbirds would scatter in the wind. Tree branches whipped and tossed. Our anticipation would build; we really believed that soon we would see a funnel, as menacing as the one in our favorite childhood movie, dancing toward us from the horizon.

Our odds were good. Oklahoma City lies in the heart of Tornado Alley, a swath of the country stretching from South Dakota to Texas. Oklahoma boasts the highest tornado wind speed ever recorded on earth: three hundred eighteen miles per hour.

At the end of our street stood an unfamiliar object—a tornado siren, a tall pole with a loudspeaker on top. It went off every Saturday morning, a regular test to ensure the siren was working. A blast at any other time meant that a twister was coming and people should take shelter.

When the siren's blare filled the neighborhood, my mother would immediately crush our hopes with a loud, "Everybody into the basement!" We pretended we didn't hear her till she finally ordered us downstairs, where she and my father stored what we considered completely useless survival supplies: radio, batteries, water, canned foods, blankets.

Though we never did get to see a cyclone, we did get to see some epic weather. Oklahoma had hail the size of golf balls that, within minutes, could put dents in your car if you left it in the driveway. Thunderclouds that dumped rain in late spring and early summer could grow to the size of skyscrapers, up to seventy thousand feet. Once, during a fierce electric storm, I looked out a window and actually saw fire in the rain: a tree branch that had been struck by lightning still ablaze while water poured down from the heavens.

That summer we moved in, my sisters and I lived mostly at the swimming pool at the end of our block. We spent the days diving off the high board, lying on our towels in the grass, and eating grilled cheese and fries at the snack bar. In late August, we three girls would lie on the trampoline in our back yard and listen to the air fill with the loud buzzing of cicadas, an elegy for the end of summer and a portent of the approach of fall and school.

When we first arrived, my sisters and I went to public school, where we were steeped in Oklahoma history. Our classes took field trips to the Cowboy Hall of Fame (since renamed the National Cowboy and Western

Heritage Museum), with its Frederic Remington paintings and sculptures. We heard stories about state icons like Will Rogers, the cowboy, performer, and humorist, and track-and-field star Jim Thorpe, a member of the Sac and Fox Nation and the first Native American to win gold for the United States in the Olympics.

Land played a huge role in the state's history and imagination, perhaps because Oklahoma is so landlocked, hemmed in by the Great Plains and hundreds of miles from the oceans, the Great Lakes, or the Gulf of Mexico. My family went boating every summer on Oklahoma's Lake Tenkiller, but it was, like almost all the rest of Oklahoma's lakes, manmade.

Celebrating the Oklahoma Land Rush was an annual school ritual. Students were urged to dress up like settlers and pose in wagons meant to look like the ones pioneers had ridden into the territory. An unfortunate photo exists of middle school me in such a wagon, wearing a long orange paisley dress and matching cap, my unruly mane of brown hair sticking out from underneath.

Years later, I heard a radio interview of a man with Native American ancestry saying how uncomfortable he was as a boy during these commemorations. In the privileged cocoon of my upbringing, it didn't dawn on me that the event we were reenacting was, as University of Oklahoma anthropology professor Daniel Swan put it, "a desperate, dark day" for Native Americans. I am ashamed of that ignorance now.

Public school came to an end the day my mother

asked my big sister, "What did you do at school today?" My sister told the truth: her class had made peanut butter cookies and watched *The Beverly Hillbillies* on TV. Suddenly, we were yanked out and put into private school.

Our new school, Casady, was an Episcopal K-through-12 academy where we wore uniforms: blue-and-white checked pleated skirts, button-up white blouses, and knee socks. The genial headmaster, Dr. Woolsey, wore roundish, wire-rimmed glasses and a bow tie and drove around campus on a golf cart. He used the word *chap*. The courses included Latin, which I took for all four years of high school.

The campus had a pretty pond with ducks and weeping willow trees along the banks, classroom buildings, playing fields, and a stone chapel. Students and teachers gathered there every morning for services complete with hymns and prayers. Once a week, if you came for an early service, you got to take communion (with real wine, unlike the Welch's grape juice at my Presbyterian church) and have sticky buns and scrambled eggs afterward at the headmaster's house next door.

A few of my fellow students complained about having to go to chapel, but I loved it. I loved starting my day in that hushed space with its vaulted ceiling, soft light streaming in through stained-glass windows. The hymns we sang, the poetic Episcopal prayers ("And we most humbly beseech thee, of thy goodness, O Lord") felt like the voice of God speaking to my young heart.

Chapel was where God prodded me when I did wrong. When I was in sixth grade and girls were starting to do things like put on makeup or necklaces bearing their boyfriends' initials, wearing a bra was an important test of how grown up you were. Girls would come up behind you in the halls and run their index fingers down your back to detect the bump of a bra strap. Being found to be braless was a great humiliation.

I was flat as a pancake. That didn't stop me from wanting to be like the girls I envied. One day, I summoned the nerve to ask my mother to take me to Penn Square Mall and buy me a bra. She took one look at me and pointed out the obvious: I didn't need one.

That rejection led to my secret plan: I saved up the money I earned helping my father mow and edge our lawn and bought one myself. I would leave home in the mornings with the bra hidden in my book bag and put it on in the school bathroom when I arrived, then take it off before I got home.

It felt thrilling when I was wearing it, every place except one: chapel. When my back rested against the hard wooden pews, I felt the metal hooks of the bra strap press against my flesh and thought, *I am lying to my mother.*

After six months of torturous guilt, I decided I must tell her. I went to her and confessed my deception. I braced for a lecture and a punishment. Instead, my mom folded me in her arms and said, "Oh, Jeannie-bug, I didn't know you wanted one that badly!" She took me to the mall that afternoon and bought me a stash of lacy white bras. Thus did chapel teach me to listen to that still, small voice of God before it becomes a megaphone.

We always ended chapel with the school song, a haunting tune with lyrics I remember word for word, decades later:

> Lord, in these quiet moments
> As we greet each new day
> Kneeling within this chapel
> Hear us all as we pray.
>
> Give us grace that we may find
> In each heart and mind
> Patience, truth and honor
> Forevermore.
>
> Lord, in those busy moments
> When we leave this altar
> When we must face life's duties
> Guide us lest we falter.
>
> We must have strength from your hand
> That this school may stand
> Always under your care.
> Grant our prayer. Amen.

My family was Presbyterian, but many of our new friends in this Bible Belt state were Baptists. I was thrilled to be invited once to see a friend's older sister get baptized; the girl, wearing a robe made of shower curtain material, was dunked in a large tank of water at the front of the church. It was so much more dramatic than the few drops of water we Presbyterians dribbled on the heads of unknowing infants!

Church was a mainstay of Oklahoma City life. It felt as if everyone I knew went to services on Sunday mornings and youth group on Wednesday nights. I sometimes ditched church with my best friend, Dixie, and headed for a nearby Bakers Square to indulge in blueberry pie instead of the catechism lectures of our Sunday school teacher. Still, the message that God loved me, that God had a purpose for me, rooted in my heart. I still have my black leather-bound Bible from those days, filled with underlines, highlighted passages, and my notes scrawled in the margins—wisdom sinking in like water into furrows.

Bible Belt rules didn't always hold firm. Southern Baptists discouraged drinking, and Oklahoma had laws restricting the sale of liquor on Sundays. In Oklahoma City, though, if an adult wanted to drink at a restaurant, all she had to do was sign a paper joining a "club" at the establishment. Conservative Christians frowned on divorce, but many of our classmates had parents who had broken up and remarried other people. When I learned once that, at that time, Oklahoma City had the second-highest divorce rate in the nation, just behind Reno, Nevada, I asked an Oklahoma native why. "The wild wind," he explained. "Something restless in the air."

Our neighbors on Hillcrest had a nightly tradition into which my parents soon settled: while we kids played outside, parents would meet up at someone's house for an evening drink. It was as loosely organized as the kids' gatherings; the grown-ups seemed to decide on the host for each night sometime during that same day. The resulting bonding worked; every time I was driven to school in Oklahoma City, it was in a carpool full of kids.

One of my favorite neighbors was Eunice Ellis, who lived two doors down with her booming-voiced husband, strapping kids, and lively dachshund dog. Mrs. Ellis had a perpetually perfect brunette hairdo and a welcoming smile; she was the lady who cooked a whole turkey once a week so that her kids' friends could always stop by for sandwiches.

On most Saturdays during football season, my parents decamped with their friends a half-hour south to Oklahoma University to watch the game. Oklahoma pride was deep and strong, and OU fandom was fervent; the Sooners were national champions in football twice during my high school years. The school's fight song, "Boomer Sooner," set to Yale's tune "Boola Boola," was so popular that one man in our neighborhood changed the horn on his car to play the melody. Word had it that another man had planned upon his death to have his coffin lined in Sooner red. Parents would leave in the morning to tailgate on ham sandwiches and Bloody Marys, watch the game, then tailgate again after. My mom and dad returned home late smelling of Joy perfume and cigars.

Our across-the-street neighbors were the Amises, a

lively family of eight: Dave Amis, his wife, Susan, and six red-haired, freckle-faced kids, three boys and three girls. They were sunny and thoroughly down-to-earth. Suzy, like me, was the middle of three sisters. She grew up to become a Ford model, an actor, an environmental advocate, and the wife of director James Cameron.

Suzy was one of several Oklahoma City people I knew who went on to fame; my high school classmate Megan Mullally became a singer and actor best known for her role as the comically blunt socialite Karen Walker in the television series *Will and Grace*. When we were in high school, I loved when Megan came to our house to practice her audition songs while my mom accompanied her on piano, Megan's gleaming voice floating out from the living room. A boy a year behind me at Casady, Clay Bennett, became a businessman, civic leader, law reformer, and head of the group that owns the NBA team the Oklahoma City Thunder.

Love of country was a mainstay, a bedrock principle. The huge park that bordered Lake Hefner in Oklahoma City was called Stars and Stripes Park and featured a patriotic-themed playground. The pavilion there has since been named for Bob Hope, who used to come with conservative stars like Anita Bryant to perform. My parents took us to a show there when I was little. I remember almost nothing except that while we were standing in a long line in the hot sun to get in, everything started to go dark. Noises sounded faint compared with the rushing in my ears. I woke up on the ground a few moments later; I had passed out from the heat. My mom revived me with a bottle of water and a box of bitter-tasting popcorn heaped with salt, which she made me eat.

I was not born in Oklahoma, but I truly did grow up there into the person I would become. It is where I am from.

My mother once told my sisters and me something self-effacing but true: "I made sure you girls had matching socks and lunch in your lunch boxes. It was your father who really raised you. He gave you your minds and souls."

Oklahoma City was like that. There, the pastor of my church, First Presbyterian Church of Oklahoma City, taught me that love is an active verb. It is something you *do*.

Oklahoma City is where my history teacher, Robert Merrick, helped us see a whole world—nations and peoples, beliefs and political structures—beyond the confines of our small classroom and the comfortable, mostly white upper-middle-class world in which I dwelled.

Oklahoma City is where I heard Casady football coach and teacher Dick McCubbin quote from Scripture, "To whom much is given, much is required." He laid out the challenge to us: You have been given everything in the world you could need or want. Now what will you do for the world?

Oklahoma City is where I learned that when a neighbor is sick, you bring dinner. When a new family moves onto your block, you welcome them with a basket of cookies and juice boxes for their kids. When a friend goes to prison, you write him and visit him at Leavenworth, and you make sure to invite the wife he left behind to every dinner party you host. My parents did this. It was an indelible lesson in loyalty and love.

On that first day in Oklahoma City, the day when I was ten years old and my family moved onto Hillcrest Avenue, my little sister, Nancy, went missing.

While movers were unloading furniture, my mother and father were directing traffic, and my big sister and I were busy claiming our bedrooms, five-year-old Nancy disappeared.

At some point, we noticed she was gone. Panic gripped me. I pictured someone taking her—a man, maybe, grasping her hand and leading her off. This is how it happens, I thought in despair: You turn around, and the person you love most in the world vanishes. You never see her again.

I started a frantic journey up the street, going house to house, asking if anyone had seen Nancy. To my relief, our new neighbors had—all of them.

She had been walking up Hillcrest Avenue, zigzag, first on one side of the street, then the other, back and forth up the block. She'd stood on tiptoe to ring the doorbell of each house. And when the grown-ups inside answered the door, she'd tilted her sunny face upward, brushing back the curls of her light brown hair. "I'm Nancy Bishop! I just moved here!"

I finally tracked her to a stately house at the end of the street. It belonged to a handsome white-haired couple named the Kennedys. When Mrs. Kennedy opened their front door, over her shoulder I could see Nancy sitting at their kitchen counter, swinging her legs happily and eating an apple.

I found Nancy that day. In the end, though, we did lose her.

Two decades later, when she was only twenty-five years old, Nancy was murdered. She and her husband, Richard, were living in Winnetka, one of Chicago's safest suburbs. They had come home from a family dinner celebrating the joyous news that Nancy was three months pregnant with what would have been their first child.

They walked through their front door to find a shadowy figure in the dark. The intruder forced them into their basement at gunpoint. There, he executed Richard with a single shot to the back of his head. The killer fired twice into Nancy's pregnant side and abdomen, then fled.

Mortally wounded, too weak to stand, Nancy picked up a tool and banged on a metal shelf to try to call for help. No help came.

When I think she must have felt her life ebbing away, the darkness closing in around her, Nancy pulled herself by her elbows along the concrete floor to where her husband lay dead. There, in her final moments, Nancy did this unimaginable thing: she drew in her blood on the floor beside him the shape of a heart and the letter *u*.

Love U.

That transcendent message of love, written by a young woman who knew she was dying, changed me forever. I started working against everything that shed more blood or created another grieving family like mine.

And it was in the heart of that fight that I found my fellow Oklahoman, Bud Welch.

CHAPTER 2

BUD

B ud Welch is a survivor—of ancestors who barely made it to Oklahoma, of tornados, of a sometimes-perilous upbringing on a farm in the wake of Oklahoma's Dust Bowl.

If you ask him to describe himself, though, Bud says simply this: he is the father of Julie Marie Welch, who died in the Oklahoma City bombing at the age of twenty-three.

I got to know Bud on a trip to Japan, where we were both invited to speak about our murdered loved ones and why we believe that more killing would dishonor their lives. The other people on the trip were a fascinating array, including Robert Meeropol, the son of Julius and Ethel Rosenberg, who in the 1950s were convicted of being Communist spies and put to death in the electric chair. Robbie was six years old at the time; he and his brother are the only children ever orphaned when the US government executed both their parents.

On the trip, Bud—in a voice a *Washington Post* reporter called "a mellow sound like tires gently coming down a gravel driveway"—told the story of his only daughter, Julie. But it wasn't the whole story. On a visit to Bud's home in Oklahoma City, I get to sit at his broad wooden kitchen table as he tells me the rest.

Bud is not just a survivor; he is a descendant of survivors.

Bud's paternal great-grandparents, James and Margaret Walsh, came to the US from Ireland out of desperation. They sailed to America after the potato famine of the late 1840s when British policies starved their country and drove more than a million Irish out. Many were too weak and malnourished to travel and died before they could escape, their mouths stained green from eating grass. The Walshes were luckier.

The couple made their way to Pennsylvania, where James Walsh dug coal in the hazardous mines around Scranton and Wilkes-Barre. The other miners mispronounced his name, calling him Welch instead of Walsh. James changed his name to fit.

Bud's great-grandmother soon saw that working in the mines was more dangerous than hunger. Life expectancy for miners like her husband was alarmingly low. "She wanted him out of coal mining," Bud relates. "Miners were nothing more than slaves then."

Bud's great-grandfather quit the mines and left for Kansas, where he got a job laboring on a farm. With an income and a place to live established, James wrote

Margaret telling her to come join him. She put a cover on a wagon and headed to Kansas by herself with their children.

Bud's grandfather, Richard Frank Welch, was only eight years old when he left in 1886 on the risky cross-country journey with his mother and siblings. The boy, known as Dick, made it to Kansas. Two of Dick's younger brothers—Bud's great-uncles—did not.

"Two little boys of my great-grandmother's died on the journey," Bud tells me. "Back then, kids got sick and died and people didn't really know what killed them." The boys were buried on the way along the rutted trail.

I take a moment to absorb that. Imagine crossing the country with small children and everything you could carry in one wagon. No GPS, no interstate, no guarantees about weather or terrain or predators along the way. Shivering at night under pale stars. Waking up to stiff joints and another day of jolting along unpaved ground. Arriving, at last, in a place as strange to you as the face of the moon, only to tell the man you love that two of the children you bore him are no more.

The Welches braved separation and death to cross the country to Kansas. They didn't remain there, though; they risked everything again to come to Oklahoma. Like thousands of others, they were lured by an irresistible promise: land on which to start a farm of their own.

Of course, the land promised was not exactly unclaimed—it had been Indian Territory guaranteed in treaties the US government made with sovereign indigenous nations, people who had been uprooted from their true home and promised a new one in what would become Oklahoma. Bud's family wandered into one of the most complex parts of the settlement of North America.

Congress had opened huge swaths of that Indian Territory to settlers through the land runs that began on April 22, 1889. Promoters ran newspaper ads and circulated flyers, many directed at immigrants like the Welches, urging people to head to the territory. The Welches settled there and started a farm, where Bud's father was born on June 6, 1907. His birth certificate states "Lincoln County, IT"—standing for "Indian Territory"— because Oklahoma was not yet a state. Oklahoma became the forty-sixth US state on November 16, 1907.

Bud's father, Emmett Frank Welch, was as much of a survivor as his ancestors. Emmett started school at the age of five. He walked to school with his sister, Gladys, age seven, from their farm several miles each day. Within three or four months into the school year, Gladys was dead. Bud's father survived.

Bud was born on the farm outside of Shawnee, Oklahoma, in 1939, just a few years after the end of the Dust Bowl that struck Oklahoma farmers hard. Drought and wild wind turned topsoil into dust that choked the earth and sky. Refugees from ravaged farms headed west looking for work—the despised and impoverished "Okies" depicted in John Steinbeck's novel *The Grapes of Wrath*.

The Welch family farm was farther east and suffered only drought, starving the crops they grew and turning their ponds for the cattle dry. Bud's father had to drill a well that is still on the farm, pumping water for thirty-five head of cattle by hand.

The Welches' farm survived. The four-hundred-eighty-acre plot is still in Bud's family.

Bud was the third of eight children and the first boy in his large Irish Catholic family. Bud was named Emmett, for his father, because the two were born on the same date, June 28. "I was born at home. When I was three or four days old, my dad said to my mom, 'Dorothy, I can't call that baby "Emmett."' To him, that was a grown person's name. So he started calling me 'Bud,' and that name stuck the rest of my life," Bud explains.

The Welches lived in a two-bedroom house, one bedroom upstairs, the other down. Bud's two youngest siblings, Kathy and Mike, slept in their parents' room, while Bud and the five other kids—Norma, Dot, Gloria, Gerarda, and Frank—slept three to a bed in two beds in the other room.

Bud survived working on the busy dairy farm from the earliest time he can remember. Bud and his father milked the cows every morning, usually around 6:00 a.m., and every evening.

Bud's first childhood memory is of helping his father feed the baby calves. "The calves of dairy cattle were taken away from their mothers the first day," Bud remembers. "You could give them milk through a nursing bucket with a rubber tit on the side, but Dad liked to teach them to drink from the bucket by themselves. I would put their little heads between my legs and put my fingers in their mouths. Any time you stick fingers in baby calves' mouths, they start sucking. So my first memory is the feeling of dipping my hands in that bucket and feeling those baby calves drinking milk through my fingers."

Bud survived driving the family pickup truck beginning when he was only five years old. On the farm was a large pasture where about sixty head of cattle grazed. They had to be brought home every night for milking. To save Bud's father the half-mile walk to the pasture, he and five-year-old Bud would drive there in a truck. Bud's father would get out and put the pickup in first gear. Tiny Bud would get behind the wheel of the truck and slowly head it down the hill while his father was outside driving the cattle.

Bud survived handing out death to living things, starting with the chickens his mother cooked for dinner. "You'd catch them, hold them with their two legs in one of your hands, holding both wings back," Bud recalls, demonstrating the grip. "You'd put their heads on a wooden block and chop their heads off. You didn't want them to get loose after that; if you did, they'd bounce and jump around for about a minute and spray blood all over you." Bud hated it.

Bud survived loading and delivering heavy milk cans for sale before he had even reached his teens. Bud's family had to haul the milk they produced into town every day, piling twenty-gallon cans into their truck and taking them to a dairy to sell. Bud's father did the milk delivery when Bud was small; Bud started driving the milk in by himself when he was only twelve.

Bud survived a tornado that whipped past his farm on May 5, 1954, when he was fourteen. The cyclone was so fierce that it sucked some of the farm's cattle off the ground and into the swirling air.

Bud describes how it started: "In the evening, I was helping Dad milk the cows when we saw this bad weather coming in from the southwest, really black clouds."

As the sky darkened, Bud's father shouted to Bud to go up to the house and check on his five younger siblings. Bud was in charge of the kids; his mother had gone into Shawnee six miles away to buy groceries.

Bud stepped onto the front porch of his house watching clouds the color of night come in from the west, with cloud-to-ground lightning striking the earth. Bud is an Oklahoman. He knew that type of storm can produce twisters, especially in the tornado season of early May. "I ran back to the barn to tell Dad to pull the cattle out of the milking machines and let them out of the stanchions [stalls where you keep cattle being milked]. I put all five kids in the basement and kept yelling for Dad to come on."

Bud's father almost didn't make it. When he came running for the house, a ferocious gust of wind shoved him to the ground. Bud's dad picked himself up and ran again, barely getting inside the house before the storm unleashed its full fury.

The tornado tore sheet iron off the hay barn. It uprooted trees in the back yard. It ripped up fences in two west pastures three-quarters of a mile from the house.

The family had cattle in those pastures. The tornado killed four head of the cattle. Fourteen-year-old Bud had to shoot two others that were near death.

"One big cow was lifted up into the air, like in the movie *Twister*. When she came back down, her right front leg was snapped off, hanging on by the skin. You can't fix a cow like that. I had to take my rifle and shoot her," Bud tells me, a haunted look flickering across his face.

The other injured cow had been impaled by a two-by-four-foot wood plank. "It was buried in her side about a foot and a half, and she was suffering," Bud says, as if he could see the dying animal still. "It was obvious she wouldn't survive. Dad was with me. He said, 'Why don't you just go ahead and kill her?' I didn't ask him to do it, because I felt bad for him. I knew good and well he didn't want to do it."

Bud survived grappling with the mysteries of life and death. It wasn't just being around the animals he got to know and then sometimes had to kill, like the hogs they raised and butchered for meat, the squirrels and rabbits and quail he hunted for food. Growing up on a farm taught him "so much about life, like where does food come from. We churned our own butter, picked our own vegetables."

Bud's morning chores usually lasted only about

an hour till he had to get to school at St. Benedict's Elementary School in Shawnee, a Catholic school run by the Sisters of Mercy. Bud started high school at St. Gregory's in tenth grade, a few years after the end of WWII. He wore khakis and lace-up shoes to school, different from the calf-high rubber boots he wore on the farm. "In the barn, the mud would get to about one foot deep. We would get a garden hose and hose them off and store them on the back porch." That's what Bud remembers most about the farm: mud. Mud, and the smell of hay and manure.

When Bud graduated high school, he took off from Oklahoma just two weeks later. His older sisters had moved to Colorado Springs the year before, and he wanted to join them. "I told Dad. He kept trying to talk me into staying, to help on the farm. I told him, 'That's the reason I don't want to stay here! I'm tired of milking cows seven days a week, every night and every morning.' So what'd I end up doing? Not long later, I'm working at a service station, seven days a week, every morning and every evening. And cows don't talk back; customers do." Bud worked a series of jobs—waiter, convenience store clerk, construction worker—till a Conoco service station hired him when he was eighteen.

In January 1958, Bud met a girl: Georgia O'Hara Branham, age sixteen. She had moved from Omaha to attend St. Mary's High School. Bud saw her at a restaurant called The Cottage near her school and fell hard. They started dating.

Georgia was an orphan. When Georgia was three months old, her father was killed on the ship the USS *West Virginia* during the 1941 Japanese attack on Pearl Harbor. Her mother died of Hodgkin's disease when Georgia was ten. "She'd been traumatized by seeing her mom get weaker and weaker. She'd never met her dad," Bud remembers. Georgia shuttled between the relatives she had left, in Colorado Springs and Omaha.

Bud turned nineteen in June; by August, he and Georgia were married. They had to marry—Georgia was three months pregnant. The couple left Colorado Springs and moved back to Bud's family farm in Shawnee in time for the baby to be born.

Bud survived the tragic end of his first child's life. Bud and Georgia's baby, a son they named Greg, was born in Shawnee in February 1959. The couple's happiness was short-lived.

"Georgia's grandmother hadn't seen Greg yet, so we went back to Colorado Springs for Easter so the grandmother could see him. On Easter Monday, Georgia and I were sleeping in before we were going to drive back to Oklahoma. The grandmother fed Greg and laid him in a baby basket in the living room," Bud says haltingly, his hands clasped on the table. "When she came back fifteen minutes later, Greg was dead."

An autopsy later revealed the baby had an unseen tumor growing in his heart. Bud was devastated. His firstborn son had died at only seven weeks old.

Bud thought he would never have children again. He

did, though: another son, Kevin, born the following year, the only one of Bud's three children still living. He and Georgia divorced in 1966 after eight years of marriage.

Bud met and married Lena Compassi, also a Catholic and native Oklahoman, a year later. By then, Bud had his own gas station on South Western Avenue in Oklahoma City. He moved to another station a mile south of Penn Square Mall, on 39th and Pennsylvania Avenue. Nancy Anthony, the head of the foundation that would end up disbursing relief funds collected for victims of the Oklahoma City bombing, used to buy gas at Bud's station years before the attack. "It was this old-style filling station. You could get your oil changed, your gas pumped."

In September 1971, Bud's daughter, Julie, was born. Bud was thirty-two years old. Even his first child's death did not prepare him for what he faced now. Julie was born prematurely, six weeks early. She weighed only a few pounds and could barely breathe; she had a condition called hyaline membrane disease, an underdevelopment of the lungs.

The disease had been made famous by Patrick Bouvier Kennedy, the youngest child of President John F. Kennedy and First Lady Jacqueline Bouvier Kennedy. Their child died in August 1963 from hyaline membrane disease at only two days old. Compounding the tragedy, his father, John F. Kennedy, was assassinated three months later. "It shook me that the Kennedy baby had died of it. A rich and powerful family, and the child still died," Bud recalls.

Julie was put in an incubator. At the time, the

survival rate for children with hyaline membrane disease was about 3 percent. Doctors gave Julie a 10 percent chance.

While Julie was being treated at Baptist Hospital in Oklahoma City, Bud remembers, "I was just talking to anyone who would listen. Just praying. I'd already lost a baby. I didn't want to lose another one."

Julie lived, but Bud was hypervigilant after he brought her home, checking on her all the time. It was the same protection he would show to her, years later, when she left for college. He called her every single day.

Bud could not foresee the death of his first child, or his last: Julie Marie Welch, who was born into this world fighting to breathe, who lived against all odds, and who died twenty-three years later in the destruction of the Murrah Federal Building.

CHAPTER 3

JULIE

Julie Marie Welch was a fighter.

You wouldn't know it from her tiny stature—she topped out at five-foot-one and about one hundred pounds. Nor would you expect it from a girl of her disposition: the girl who went to Mass every day during the last two years of her life.

Her feisty nature was apparent early. Bud remembers the resistance. "She and I used to really tangle, until she was about five or six years old. I wanted her to do something and she wouldn't do it. I finally figured out that there were some things that she just wasn't going to do. Some things you could change her mind on, but other things, no. My problem was recognizing which ones," Bud says of his daughter.

How did Bud learn to recognize the ones where Julie wouldn't budge? I ask him. "By living through the hell that came otherwise!" he replies, laughing. "We were afraid she would be weak, but she turned out just the opposite."

Julie was a fighter for her friends. When she was little, some classmates teased her about her small size and her name, calling her "Grape Juice" because of her last name, Welch. She didn't put up with put-downs; she encouraged other kids not to either. "I remember a time or two Julie had told other kids they needed to not physically hit back but to stick up for themselves," Bud says. "Because if someone ever tried to bully Julie, she wouldn't tolerate it. She'd get up in their face and make it real clear she wasn't going to put up with that."

Julie was a protector of the small and weak. When Julie was in elementary school, her half brother Kevin brought two puppies up from Mississippi, where he was living, and gave one each to Julie and Bud. "The puppies were in the back yard playing with something, just wallering this baby robin all over the grass," Bud tells me, motioning out the window to the green lawn outside.

"What is 'wallering'?" I ask, needing a translation from Oklahoma farm-speak to English. I learn that wallering is what buffalo did in the "wallers," small ponds of mud on the farm where the creatures could poke around to cool off.

Julie took the tiny bird and made it her pet. Bud smiles as he tells me the name she gave it: Jellybean. "It stayed in the house and got to flying in there. It would get up on the windowsills and just s— all over the place."

The bird got to be too much even for Bud's kind and patient wife, Lois. She insisted on turning the robin loose. Bud, Lois, her son Chris, and Julie all took

Jellybean out to the nature center to let him go. The bird perched on Bud's finger until Bud finally shook him off. The bird flitted to a nearby branch, then went no farther, as if he didn't want to leave Julie, the little girl who had cared for him. "She went to crying. I went to crying," Bud recalls, half laughing. "Chris looked at both of us like we were crazy."

Julie Welch was the best kind of fighter—the one who is, underneath, softhearted. Once, her beloved dog Duffy was run over in the driveway and killed. Julie had to go to school the same day and have her official school picture taken. Julie's mother remembered how puffy Julie's eyes were in that photo, from crying over her dog.

Julie was a protector of her mom, Lena, who bore some emotional scars from a difficult childhood with her own mother. Lena's mother suffered from depression and raised Lena in a house full of trash and unwashed dishes. Lena learned young how to try to clean the house herself. She never invited friends over.

Lena and Bud divorced in 1977 when Julie was six; a "good divorce," Bud says. They hired one attorney and agreed on everything. Lena got the house, all the furniture, and child support. Bud paid Julie's school tuition when she started attending a private Catholic high school. Julie lived with her mother until college but kept close to Bud. She would stay with him on weekends, and he would take her on spring break trips.

"Julie mentioned a few times to me, 'I worry about Mom,' and I'd say, 'Mom's going to be okay.' I assured

Julie that her mom would never need anything that would not be provided," Bud says. Lena always, only, spoke well of him.

Julie's mother, Lena, died of a stroke on September 13, 2018, the day after what would have been Julie's forty-seventh birthday. After Lena's death, Bud was torn up. "I keep thinking how Julie was always protective of her mom. But Julie couldn't protect her mom because she wasn't there to be with her."

Julie was an advocate for those who needed help. She discovered a way she could give people that help: by speaking their language.

Julie attended public schools until ninth grade, then went to Bishop McGuinness, a private Catholic school, for high school. There, Julie befriended a girl who had moved from Mexico and had quickly picked up English. The girl's ability to learn a new language seemed to Julie to be a magical power that humans could possess. Julie started studying every foreign language she could and found that she was good at it. She spent her junior year as an exchange student in Spain, polishing the language skills that eventually got her hired as a translator for the Social Security Administration in the Murrah building.

Julie started interpreting for Spanish speakers as early as high school. Julie's grandfather, Bud's dad, asked her to translate for some of his neighbors whose families had come to Oklahoma from Mexico. One of them, a seventy-five-year-old woman who lived a half mile from Bud's family farm, was being threatened with deportation. "She had been born at home—a lot of people were at that time—so there was no birth certificate," Bud explains.

Bud's dad brought the woman and her family to Bud's Texaco station to meet Julie, who accompanied them to the immigration office near I-40 and Meridian in Oklahoma City. It was a success. Immigration authorities gave the woman a green card, then determined that she was in fact a US citizen because she had been born in Oklahoma.

Julie's grandfather was elated. "She was just the apple of his eye," Bud says. Bud is glad his father died two years before Julie lost her life in the bombing. "If he'd have been alive when she died, it would have killed him."

Bud worried about his daughter when she started smoking cigarettes (and the occasional marijuana blunt) in high school. "I got onto her about that. Her mom was a smoker, I was a smoker. But she was born with her lungs underdeveloped." Bud was relieved when she finally quit in college.

When the time came for Julie to think about college, Bud, who had never gone past high school, bought a couple of college guides and started looking through them with her. She applied to five Jesuit colleges—Marquette, Loyola University Chicago, Boston College, Fordham, and St. Louis University—and got into them all. Marquette offered her a foreign language scholarship when she scored the highest among ninety-five applicants in the scholarship competition.

Once Julie had chosen Marquette, she was ready to go. One day, she drove to Bud's gas station in her mom's Oldsmobile Cutlass, announcing that she needed his truck immediately to start packing. Her scheduled drop-off at college was a week away. Julie packed Bud's blue-and-silver GMC Jimmy to the roof, leaving what Bud calls "one little itty-bitty place" for his suitcase. "A freshman, especially a girl, takes every damn thing they own to school."

A week later, the two drove from Oklahoma City to Milwaukee, home of Marquette University. Bud helped move Julie into her dormitory, McCormick, nicknamed The Beer Can for its shape: round and twelve stories high. ("What else is round and contains twelve ounces in Milwaukee but a beer can?" Bud asks me, laughing.)

"The priest had us unload everything out front. I reached into the truck and got this little teddy bear, one foot long, given by an aunt on Julie's first birthday. She slept with it every night of her entire life," Bud remembers. He handed the stuffed animal to Julie. She threw it back into the truck and told him, "Don't put that damn bear out here!" Bud was ready to close the tailgate when she crawled in, retrieved the teddy bear from the floorboard, wrapped the bear in a towel, and placed it gently on the ground.

"I figured out what was going on: she didn't want anyone to know about this bear. She found out by sunset that about 98 percent of girls and half the young men had their stuffed animals too." The bear was buried with Julie in her casket when she died.

Julie was a fighter for her beliefs. During her freshman year at Marquette, Julie opposed the deployment of US troops to the Gulf War. Julie and some other students made an anti-war banner and put it on the school lawn. The school's priests made them remove it.

"Julie took the banner and put it up in her window. They tried to get her to take it down. She wouldn't take it down. They figured out she was never going to do it, and let it go. The ironic thing is," Bud observes, "she opposed that war, and that war would a few years later kill her." Timothy McVeigh met his bombing coconspirators Terry Nichols and Michael Fortier when they were soldiers in the same unit during the war.

Julie spent a year of college in Spain attending the University of Madrid. She walked to school. "Every day, she had to go three blocks out of her way, to go around the naval base, because of the Basque bombings. So she survived living in Madrid and came back to Oklahoma City and perished," Bud observes, his voice edged with disbelief.

Julie was a fighter for the vulnerable. In her freshman year of college, a dean asked her to interpret for some priests and lay people on a mission trip in the Dominican Republic.

"She stayed with a family about six miles from the Haitian border," Bud recounts. "There was a conflict back then between Dominicans and Haitians; crime was coming across the border. Julie, the trip director, and one priest stayed with a woman and her five kids. They lived in a shack with a dirt floor and no indoor toilet. The woman's husband had been killed a few years before.

"Julie was just devastated by the way the family had to live. The father had been the breadwinner. Julie was really crazy about the oldest kid in the family, a fifteen-year-old girl. Julie wanted the girl to come back with her. 'You can live with my dad. He will take care of you,' Julie told her. The director said to Julie, 'You can't.' She got in a big argument with him."

Julie navigated danger successfully, almost unthinkingly. When she and two other girls went on vacation traveling through Italy on a tight budget, they put up a tent in a public park in Rome and slept there outside.

Still, Bud called Julie every night when she was in college, sometimes just for thirty seconds. He did it to check in, to make sure she was okay. "I could tell if she had some issues going on," he recalls. "If she didn't, she called me 'Dad.' If she did, she called me 'Daddy.'"

Julie was a fighter for her vision of her future. When Julie graduated Marquette in May 1994, she was fluent in five languages, including Spanish, Italian, and French. The morning Bud and Julie were leaving Milwaukee after graduation, the dean of the language department made Julie an offer: stay on to teach Spanish as a paid graduate assistant and get a master's degree tuition-free.

Julie turned it down, saying that she wanted to go back to Oklahoma City to work for a couple of years and be with her family. Bud tried to argue her out of it. "I wanted her to go back to Marquette in the fall, where she would get a stipend, live rent free on campus, eat free in the cafeteria, no living expenses, no tuition. I thought that was a hell of a deal. We had several spats about it driving home."

Julie, the fighter, won the fight. Bud reflects, "I thought, you've got to let her make her decision. If I influence her too much, she won't feel right about the decision she made."

Back home in Oklahoma City, Julie found out the Social Security Administration was hiring and got a job as an interpreter, a position she had held for less than nine months when she was killed.

I have to ask Bud: Did he look back after her death and think, *If you'd just listened to me, you'd still be alive?* Bud is quick to say yes. "I went through all of that, some anger toward Julie after her death, because if she'd done what I wanted her to do, she wouldn't have been there [in the Murrah building]. Then I was angry at myself, because I had encouraged her to continue her Spanish. You're just searching for a reason why this wouldn't have happened if you had done something different."

Her former college roommate remembered a Julie who changed dramatically during her school years, into someone who was becoming more and more serious about her faith. When Julie's school friends traveled from around the country to attend her funeral, held in a church, they joked later that Julie had always vowed to get them there, into a house of God.

During the last two years of her life, Julie became a daily communicant—someone who goes to church every day to take the bread and cup. I asked a Catholic friend why anyone, especially a young woman in her early twenties with a busy life, would want to do this. "Because you want more Jesus in you," my friend replied simply.

Julie was going to Mass in the mornings before work at St. Charles Borromeo Church on NW 50th Street, or after work in the evenings at St. Therese of the Little Flower downtown. She especially loved Little Flower, a church where Mass was said in Spanish for the congregation of mostly immigrants.

Just before she died, Julie started a program at Little Flower for preschoolers who had come from Mexico knowing little English. Playing with this gentle young woman who spoke a language familiar to them reassured the children. Bud remembers meeting Julie at the church for Mass; when she approached, kids came running across the street toward her, calling her name.

Because Julie had to be at work by 8:00 a.m., she usually attended the 7:00 a.m. service when she went to Mass in the morning. The service lasted thirty minutes, allowing her to get to her office on the first floor of the Murrah building on time.

Julie and Bud started a routine of meeting for lunch once a week, typically on a Wednesday. She had only a half-hour lunch break. They ate at a Greek restaurant across the street from Julie's office, next to the Water Resources Building, where a tape recording of an administrative hearing would capture the boom of the explosion on the day of the bombing.

Julie would call the restaurant ahead of time and order food for herself and Bud. "I'd pull up on 5th Street and wait till she walked out from the Murrah building. Julie had thirty minutes for lunch, and she wouldn't take thirty-one. She loved her job and wanted to stick to all the rules," Bud tells me, his voice tinged with pride.

Julie had another reason for choosing that location: she wanted to walk to lunch to avoid moving her car out of the employee parking lot. She didn't want to lose the precious spot she tried to snag each morning under the shade of the lone, spreading tree in the lot.

I know why: if you park your car in the summer sun in Oklahoma, you will be greeted by a furnace blast of heat when you return. I worked in Oklahoma City the summer after my first year of law school, at a firm whose partners included the son of the man for whom the Murrah Federal Building was named. I started the morning with hair and makeup neatly done, only to have it all wilt when I stepped into the oven-like temperature of my car.

"On hot days, she tried to get under that tree," Bud tells me. "On the day of the bombing, her car was parked one row away. The windows were blown out. The top of the car, hood, and trunk were caved in from pressure."

After the bombing, the FBI tore apart every car in the lot, including Julie's, looking for detonators. The FBI considered cutting down the tree, too, to examine shrapnel embedded in the wood. Bud argued that the tree had withstood the explosion and ought to be allowed to live. In the end, the tree was saved.

The elm, known as the Survivor Tree, still stands. Bud took me to see it, at the Oklahoma City National Memorial and Museum. We rested in its shade while a breeze lifted its branches—a place of solace for Bud, his communion with Julie. She had stood there too.

Julie was a protector, a rescuer. Her heart pulled her toward those in need, and she fought to help them.

I know what it is like to need someone with a heart like Julie's. Someone rescued me once when I should have died. It happened when I was nineteen years old, only a little younger than Julie.

I was in my sophomore year at Northwestern University's Medill School of Journalism. That was the year we were all to go out during the winter term and work as reporters at real daily newspapers. The program was called Teaching Newspaper. The papers got free labor; we got our bylines over clips that showed we could report and write a good story.

I headed for a place I thought would be warm during those winter months: Macon, Georgia. Instead, it was cold, and the room in the dilapidated apartment I rented didn't have central heating.

What it had was a space heater, an old one, open

flames burning against ceramic tile. It looked quaint. It warmed my small bedroom well enough. What I didn't know, in my college-girl ignorance, was that it was emitting an odorless, colorless gas that could kill me: carbon monoxide.

This was in the days before carbon monoxide and smoke detectors were standard equipment in every living space. It simply wasn't on my radar screen. I should have been wary, since just about every other thing in the apartment was broken: the refrigerator that barely kept food lukewarm and leaked water all over the kitchen floor, the overhead electrical fixtures that didn't work.

I was gone during the day, at the newspaper office or out in the field. I would come back at night, turn on the gas in the heater, close the door to my room, and go to sleep. I would wake in the morning dizzy, headachy, wobbly, and weak. I thought I was coming down with something. As the days went by, it got worse. Some mornings, I would get out of bed only to fall to the floor, my head banging against the hardwood. I would lie there, barely able to move, thinking, *Something is wrong with me.*

One day, I did something I rarely ever do: I called in sick. I phoned the newspaper and told them I wasn't feeling well and was going to spend the day in bed. Then I went back to my bedroom, the room where the space heater was spewing carbon monoxide, and closed the door.

That room should have been my tomb. I should have died there, at age nineteen. Instead, a miracle happened: Pam came. She rescued me.

Pam was a woman who worked at the paper. She was friendly, as they all were in their Southern way, but she wasn't exactly a friend. Something prompted her to do what coworkers almost never do: she came in the middle of the day to check on me.

The unlikelihood of that stuns me. Who does that? Who hears that a coworker is sick and goes to her home midday to see if she is all right?

Pam knocked on the door and heard me struggling to get out of bed and falling to the floor. I landed against the heater. Its flames started burning the skin off my upper right arm. I was so far gone, I didn't even feel it; I lay there motionless as fire turned my skin into charred paperlike shreds.

Pam managed to get into the apartment—how, again, I wonder—and told me later that when she opened the door to my room, she felt a whooshing sensation: oxygen rushing into a tiny room where there was none, where the air was dead.

Pam carried me out and took me to her doctor, who immediately sent me to the emergency room.

It took skin grafts and plastic surgery to repair the damage. My nineteen-year-old self was devastated at what she saw in the mirror. The mark—a foot-long scar— would always be there, obvious in all but long sleeves. Who would ever love her?

Soon after I returned to school, when everyone seemed to have heard the news of my accident, I discovered something astonishing, a hidden blessing of my burn. Outwardly perfect students who secretly knew they were imperfect too started coming to me in confidence, one by one. A tennis player who was developing arthritis that could jeopardize her athletic career at the school if her coach found out. A sorority sister who could not straighten one of her arms; she held it in a pose that looked elegant but was meant to mask her limitation. I was living proof to them that they were not alone.

My arm still bears that scar. Now I see it as a sign of life. I am alive, by the grace of God. It is a permanent reminder of what I owe to Pam—every day I have lived since then. She would deny this, but I call her an angel. She was a mere mortal. But a voice told her to come to me that day, and she listened.

A panel in the Oklahoma City Memorial Museum states, "Survivors often speak to the unexplainable of April 19, 1995. Seemingly meaningless decisions and changes in routine at 9:02 a.m.—in the Murrah and other bombed buildings—make the difference between life and death."

I think of Julie Marie Welch on April 19, 1995, and wrestle with this mystery: Where was Julie's Pam, the person who should have felt that prompting to call Julie over and talk to her for a minute in the back, or act on a sudden impulse to ask her to meet for a 9:00 a.m. coffee across the street? If that had happened, Julie would have lived.

Yet part of me thinks I know the answer to that why: Because Julie *was* Pam. Julie was the fighter for others, the lover of birds and puppies and children. She was the one who would reach out to you, who would speak up for you, who would pray for you. She was the one who would come to save you.

CHAPTER 4

BILL

Bill McVeigh is the quiet man who plants things and makes them grow.

Bill, the father of Timothy McVeigh, is a man who belongs to things. He has, at various times in his life, belonged to a childhood drum corps; neighborhood kids' sports teams; a volunteer fire company; a union, the United Auto Workers; a church; the army; bowling and golf leagues; an American Legion hall; men's softball teams; and the Eagles Club. He still belongs to many of them. He is a joiner, a doer, a helper.

He is a man as firmly rooted in his community as the corn he grows is grounded in the soil of western New York, where he grew up. Except for his two years in Fort Campbell, Kentucky, serving in the army during the Vietnam War, Bill has spent his entire life within the five-mile perimeter of Lockport and Pendleton, New York, outside of Buffalo. Bill has never lived anywhere else. He has never wanted to.

Drive around with Bill McVeigh, and he can tell you how every mound of dirt was formed, how tall the trees used to be on a certain hill, what crops were grown in a field. He will take you for red hots and milkshakes at Reid's, the same roadside diner he has eaten at since he was a boy. He can show you every house where he has ever lived, starting with the small yellow farmhouse where he was born.

Bill has lunch once a month with friends who graduated from his Catholic high school with him in 1957. The guy who started it has known Bill since first grade. Bill's regular poker game has existed for decades, quarter poker with a seventy-five-cent limit on bets. The friends gather and eat Jim's goulash, or Bill's chili, made with half hamburger and half hot sausage. There is a waiting list to get in.

Bill grew up in Lockport, named for the set of locks for the Erie Canal that winds through the center of the city. Through those locks, the canal climbs the Niagara Escarpment, a sudden rise where the Niagara River crosses and surges into the Niagara Falls.

The locks were built mostly by Scottish and Irish immigrants, who came for the work and stayed. Bill's grandparents, Hugh and Wilhelmina McVeigh, started a farm at the top of one of the huge hills of dirt dug up by the canal. Bill's father, Edward William McVeigh, was one of five children, all born on the farm. Bill was named for him, William Edward.

Bill is one of two sons. Bill asked me not to talk

much about his younger brother. "He wants just not to be known," Bill says.

Pendleton, a rural area outside of Lockport where Bill lives now, is a town of working people. You're more likely to find a John Deere riding mower in front of a house than an expensive car. Bill and his friends head to a diner in next-door Lockport for the fish fry on Fridays, or beef on weck other days of the week. The middle-aged waitress knows all the men by name.

American flags are everywhere. Every day at noon and at midnight since the September 11, 2001, attacks, the local radio station, WYRK, plays a different recording of "The Star-Spangled Banner." Bill was driving me through the town when the song happened to come on his car radio, this steadfast expression of patriotism in response to terror.

The parking lot at the public golf course where Bill plays is full of GM trucks, almost identical side by side. You won't find a single foreign car in the lot. Inside the clubhouse, the guy behind the bar is also the one who tends the grounds and owns the place.

Author Joyce Carol Oates, who was born in Lockport, described the McVeighs' hometown in an essay published shortly after the Oklahoma City bombing: "Pendleton is barely even a town, lacking its own post office, commercial center and coherent identity. It's more a region than a community, farmland interspersed with ranch houses of modest dimensions, often with flagpoles in the front yards (as in front of the McVeigh family's home). Here and there are remains of old, weatherworn farmhouses, perhaps an old, rotted barn, coop or silo—relics of an era so seemingly remote in 1995 that they might be from another century."

Bill's father grew up on his dad's farm but went to work at the Harrison foundry in Lockport when he came of age. He stayed there for thirty years.

Bill's mother, Angela, was in a wheelchair for Bill's entire childhood, stricken by multiple sclerosis. The family would take her out on Saturdays, her one night out, to the fire department parades in the towns around Lockport. Bill and his little brother played in the drum corps. Firefighters saved a place for Bill's father to park his car in the midway, so that people could stop by and say hello to Bill's mother, and her boys could bring her a cup of chowder. Angela McVeigh lived long enough to know her grandson, Timothy, who was four years old when she died.

Maybe it was because Bill's father was working and his mother couldn't go outside and play with her boys. Maybe it is Bill's innate kindness, his affable nature, his unpretentiousness. Whatever the reason, Bill's life, from the start, has been spent in the close and constant company of friends.

It began on the farm where Bill and his little brother were raised, in a small house next door to their grandparents' larger one. Bill, his brother, and their friends "were over there basically all the time," Bill tells me as he points out the house. "We'd go in the barn a lot. In winter, they had this old county ditch. It'd freeze over and we'd skate forever. When ice wasn't good to skate, we'd go sledding, down a great big mound of dirt near an old bridge where my grandfather's toolshed was."

Bill and his brother turned one of the farm's hay fields into a baseball diamond, where they played with friends—their own field of dreams. "We used a piece of wood for the backstop. We had the official length for the bases. We had everything measured out," Bill says. There were no umpires, no coaches, no uniforms, no parental or professional organizers—just boys, on their own, playing.

Bill and his childhood friends put together the same pickup teams for football and basketball. For the latter, farm kids like Bill would practice in a gym so broken down that holes in the roof would let in the snow that regularly blanketed the town. The boys simply swept the snow off the court and played. "We were farmers; we learned to play basketball in a barn," Bill says with a shrug. The boys found a wood floor in Bill's grandfather's barn where the hay used to be, put baskets up on both ends, and played full court.

Bill learned young to work hard, in a large garden plot owned by his father behind his grandparents' house. "Make sure these two rows of corn are hoed today," Bill remembers his dad saying. "That's how I grew up, from the age of six or seven." Bill and his little brother sold vegetables on the side of the road at a small farm stand in front of their house. At the end of the season, Bill's family split the money four ways: Mom, Dad, Bill, and his brother.

"Paul's Bakery would come three times a week with bread in a basket, coffee cake, or rolls. That's what my mom would use her money for," Bill remembers. Bill used his share of earnings for candy, pop, and football cards sold at a store up the road. At night, he would nestle on a couch and listen to Yankees games on the radio with his grandfather, who sat nearby smoking a pipe.

Bill's parents, deeply rooted Catholics, sent him and his little brother to Catholic schools, first to elementary school at St. Patrick's, a boys' school in Lockport, then to DeSales Catholic High School, a small school where most of the teachers were priests.

Bill's little brother went on to college, but Bill didn't, choosing instead to follow in his father's footsteps to work at the Harrison Radiator plant in Lockport, manufacturing parts for General Motors. Bill worked there his whole adult life, starting on March 13, 1963, at age twenty-three.

That same month, he met a pretty girl at a Catholic bowling league, Mildred (nicknamed Mickey) Hill. She lived in a nearby town on the Niagara Escarpment called Pekin—the same name as the city where my father grew up in downstate Illinois. Bill asked Mickey on a date, to the bowling banquet. Within months, though, Bill was drafted to serve in the Vietnam War.

Bill entered the army on August 24, 1963. He did basic training at Fort Dix and the rest of his service at

Fort Campbell, Kentucky, where he drove an eighteen-wheeler truck. "We drove the 101st Airborne guys to the planes. After they'd jump, we'd go out to the jump zone and pick them up, take them back to their barracks. A lot of 'em didn't come back from Vietnam. They were all infantry. One reserve guy told me later that, of his whole division, he was the only one who came back," Bill says.

Bill never had to go overseas to fight, he thinks because of his mom. "They ask you if there is any reason you would have to go home in an emergency. I told them about my mother. She got bad right before I went into the service. She was in the hospital then, and the doctor told my dad twice she wouldn't make it."

When his service ended, Bill came back to the radiator plant in Lockport. He married Mickey soon after, in August 1965. They had their first child, a girl, exactly nine months later. Their middle child, Timothy, was born on April 23, 1968. The birth of Jennifer, the last of their children, followed in 1974.

The marriage foundered. When Tim was around eleven years old, Mickey told Bill she was leaving him. Tim's sisters went with their mother, but Tim wanted to stay with Bill. When Mickey moved out of state with their two daughters, Bill started working the night shift at the plant so he could be there during the day for Tim.

The couple reunited for a time but split again, finally divorcing in 1984, five years after Mickey had first said goodbye. Tim stayed with Bill, who kept working nights so he could take Tim to and from school and make him dinner in the evenings.

Bill and his night shift coworkers got off work early in the morning, around 6:30 a.m. Most days, they would go home, get their kids off to school, then sleep. Once a week, though, after the school drop-off, the men met at the bowling alley or golf course around 8:00 a.m. to play and have a beer after.

Bill and those friends have stayed close. Bill's bowling league, the Midnight Bombers (named for the midnight shift), and his golf league are still in existence. To this day, Bill organizes the annual tournaments for them both.

The men he plays with count on him to do it: Bill is a math guy. In grade school, when his teacher read out math problems, Bill raised his hand with the answer before she had even finished the question. Bill can take a league of players and figure out handicaps, how to split the course or lane fees, and how to award the prize money at the end of a tournament. Until recently, he had his own office in the basement of Lockport's American Legion hall, doing the books that tally up the income and expenses from the bar, the pull-tabs, and special events like the ham raffle or lasagna dinner.

Bill has spent his life doing things you cannot do alone, that you can do only in the company of other people. He pitched on a softball team sponsored by a local bar. He coached Little League, including his son Tim's childhood baseball team, the Senators. He helped run the regular bingo game at his church, Good Shepherd.

Bill's kids went to church every Sunday growing up. "It was a rite of passage," Bill says. "You went to church on Sunday; they went too." Timothy McVeigh, like his older sister before him, was confirmed in the Catholic Church when he was a junior in high school.

I go with Bill to his church, Good Shepherd, for a Sunday morning Mass in summer. The church is red brick outside but cream colored and light within. The sanctuary is full of mostly older people. The women wear printed blouses and slacks; the leather-skinned men are dressed in T-shirts and pants or shorts. Everyone has his or her regular spot.

Bill knows the words to all the prayers; you can tell it is a comforting routine for him. He comes early, before the pews fill up, and listens to the music being rehearsed by the keyboard player and cantor. Bill tells me that this is a time he thinks of Tim. "But I think about him all the time," Bill adds quietly.

Over Bill's shoulder, I can see images all along the wall to my right: stark depictions of Jesus being arrested, whipped, mocked, tortured, crucified—then his broken body being taken down and laid in a tomb. These are the stations of the cross, the ones the faithful walk and pray beneath to enter into those moments of Jesus' suffering and death.

I look back at Bill, and it strikes me: *I am sitting in the house of a God whose only son was executed, beside a father who knows what it is like to have his only son put to death.*

After Mass, Bill leads me past the shady grass under

tall trees where the church's lawn fete is held every summer. He shows me the empty space in the church cemetery where he will be buried someday. Some of the gravestones around the plot have special markings recognizing military veterans buried there, mostly from the two World Wars and Korea. I observe out loud that Tim could get this recognition if he were buried there. Bill says that is true; his son has not been stripped of his status as a veteran.

The year he was confirmed, Tim was getting by in school and working part time at a Burger King. After his high school graduation, though, Tim struggled to find his feet. He quit Burger King. He tried a business college but quit that too, only to return to work at a different Burger King restaurant, the best job he could find. In the changing economy of western New York in the 1980s, the Harrison plant wasn't hiring.

Two years after graduating from high school, Tim was still working low-wage jobs. Bill says that one night, "he come home and said, 'Dad, I'm going in the army.' I says, 'Good, when?' He says, 'Tomorrow.' Never told me ahead of time. He took care of everything himself. When Tim joined the military, it didn't bother me. It was something for him to do to keep him going."

A son going off to the army is not unusual in a place like Lockport the way it is in the suburb where I live. My son Brendan is one of the few people you see in uniform when he returns home from school at the US Naval Academy. But a town like Lockport is built on people like

Bill who quietly serve the church, serve their volunteer fire company, serve their community in a thousand ways. It is a familiar thing in a place like that to serve one's country.

"I wasn't worried about him when he come home from Iraq," Bill confesses as we sit at his kitchen table at dusk. "I was really worried when he was there. I was thinking about it all the time. When he got home from war, that's when I thought I could breathe easy."

Bill's gaze shifts to the window, the setting sun bathing his face. How wrong he turned out to be.

CHAPTER 5

TIM

Timothy McVeigh was unremarkable.

He was bright, but a so-so student. He was never a star athlete.

He never distinguished himself in the community as the hardest worker or most willing volunteer. Tim's life was small, like the bedroom in Bill's house he once occupied.

But neither was the young Timothy McVeigh a troublemaker, one who did disturbing, violent things. He was not known as a delinquent by the police. No neighbor or teacher who knew him at a young age would ever say of him, "I always knew he would turn out this way."

On the contrary, as fellow Lockport native Joyce Carol Oates noted in a *New Yorker* essay, Tim "had an undistinguished, virtually anonymous career" growing up in school. James Allen, who was the vice principal and the school disciplinarian of Starpoint Central School when Tim graduated high school in 1986, told the *New*

York Times that "what everybody remembers is that he was never any problem."

One reporter wrote shortly after the bombing that people who knew the young Timothy McVeigh said he was indistinguishable from everyone else; even the problems he experienced, such as his parents' divorce, were average.

Timothy McVeigh was unlike David Biro, the teenager who murdered my sister Nancy, her husband, and their unborn baby. David had sent up a hundred red flags during his childhood. He had shot at people through his window with a BB gun. He had killed animals with that same gun—birds and squirrels, shooting them in the head so they couldn't run away. David had burglarized his high school and stolen $15,000 worth of computer equipment, brazenly leaving it in the open in his bedroom for anyone to see. He had tried to sicken his own family by tainting their milk with rat poison.

Timothy McVeigh did nothing like that. He helped run the kids' games at the Good Shepherd Church lawn fete. He invited his school-aged friends over for snacks and a swim in the McVeighs' backyard, aboveground pool at their house on Meyer Road. He babysat for neighbors.

When he was a teen, Tim occasionally helped around the house he shared with Bill, pouring concrete on the basement floor to fix cracks in it without having been asked. Tim put on a new storm door. He never worked in Bill's garden, but he helped blow snow in the winter and mow in summer. He would do normal things, sitting with Bill and watching TV in the living room, Tim on the couch on the south wall and Bill in the big chair in the corner.

Tim put up the original flagpole that stood in front of Bill's house. That pole is no longer there; it had been made of steel and had rusted. Bill had to dig it up years later when Tim was either in the army or in prison and replace it with the aluminum flagpole that now stands in the front yard. Bill flies the American flag on that pole every day from mid-May till after Veterans Day in November.

Timothy McVeigh was not the Bad Seed, the protagonist of the play that haunted me when I was young.

My mom performed in local theater, so we always had scripts of plays around the house. I loved reading them, especially the collected plays of a single writer: Lillian Hellman, Shakespeare, George Bernard Shaw.

The play that scared me most was *The Bad Seed*, about a little girl who was anything but unremarkable. She was evil. She plotted and manipulated and lied and, ultimately, killed, until even the girl's disbelieving mother grasped that her child was capable of murder.

Timothy McVeigh, both as a child and as a teenager, showed no trace of that.

There were some tremors: he was deeply affected as a child when his mother packed her bags and left Bill, for the first of what would be several departures before she finally divorced him. In his early teens, Tim started describing himself as a survivalist, stockpiling food and water in the event of an invasion. Two big blue barrels of water Tim had procured were still in Bill's basement when I visited, evidence of a fear of being attacked rather than a plan to attack others. The young Timothy McVeigh showed no violence toward people, no outward manifestations of hate.

It would be tempting to say that Bill, as Tim's father, should have seen some warning sign of what was to come. He didn't. No one did.

After the bombing, Bill did get five or six hateful letters saying that if he had brought Tim up right, his son's terrorist strike never would have happened. Bill's response: "All my neighbors knew me, they knew him, they didn't see this coming. The people at Tim's school—no one saw it coming. He won medals, the Bronze Star. When [US General Norman] Schwarzkopf met with Saddam Hussein's officers [to sign an armistice agreement after Desert Storm], they picked Tim as one of the guards patrolling the building. So the army didn't see it coming either."

Bill can name only one warning sign in Tim's childhood and young adulthood: Tim's fixation with guns.

Bill has never cared much for guns. He has never been to a gun show; he never brought Tim to one as a child. Bill did some pheasant hunting growing up but never took Tim hunting. Once, though, when Tim was ten years old, Bill's father let Tim shoot his .22-caliber rifle. Tim loved it instantly.

"I believe that's why he went into the army," Bill told

me. "He just wanted to shoot. He loved to shoot guns." A former coworker of Tim's confirmed that belief; he told a reporter that when he had asked Tim why he wanted to go in the army, Tim had answered, "You get to shoot."

Bill took me out to his back yard to show me the place where Tim would practice shooting at targets he created out of metal and wood. "It bothered the hell out of the neighbors," Bill told me. "One guy ran up to Tim, said, 'You can't be shooting out here.' Tim called the sheriff and found out what his rights were. Found out he couldn't shoot here—so he and a friend bought a lot in the hunting country, the southern tier of New York state, just so they could have someplace to shoot."

That friend was Dave Darlak, who had known Tim since high school. Together, in January 1988, when Tim was only nineteen, they bought ten acres of wooded land southeast of Buffalo, paying the $7,000 price in monthly installments from their paychecks. A neighbor told *The Washington Post* later that he remembered hearing the sounds of gunfire and explosives from the land for up to five hours per day.

Bill's father had owned four hunting guns: two double-barrels, a pump, and an automatic. Bill had no interest in them, intending to sell them at a garage sale after his father died. Bill's only gun had been won in an Eagles Club raffle; it sat unused. "Timmy took 'em to a gun show in Michigan. Come back and had sold them all. That's how I knew he was into guns," Bill said.

Bill led me down to the basement of the house he

had shared with Tim and showed me the metal locker where Tim had stored his guns and ammunition. "Tim's cabinet," Bill calls it. He hadn't paid much attention to it until the FBI came to search the house.

The door of the shed is plastered with black and yellow stickers. Two stickers bear a skull and crossbones. One is captioned: "Is there life after death? Trespass here and find out." The other reads, "There is nothing in here worth your life." A third sticker proclaims, in bold print, "WARNING! TRESPASSERS WILL BE SHOT. SURVIVORS WILL BE SHOT AGAIN."

The messages on those stickers reveal something about the Timothy McVeigh who would one day build a truck bomb and drive it to Oklahoma City; they express not only a fear of attack but a determination to counter-attack.

I got another clue to the mystery of Timothy McVeigh when Bill took me to the Wendelville Fire Company chowder fundraiser in nearby North Tonawanda, New York, on a bright summer day. Volunteer firefighters stirred huge pots of soup in the parking lot behind the firehouse. Steam rose over the dark broth as the rich aroma of chicken, potatoes, corn, and carrots floated into the warm air.

Men and women, mostly gray-haired and weather-worn, lined up with plastic coolers and oversized glass jars to buy the chowder. They bid on raffle baskets of trinkets displayed on nearby tables, all to help the fire company purchase a new truck or some lifesaving equipment.

I looked at them and thought, *This is what "the salt of the earth" means. These are the ones who keep us from rotting, who preserve what is good.*

But I had this thought too: *It must not have been enough for Timothy McVeigh.* The small town, the daily humdrum. It must not have been enough to hold Tim, much less lure him.

Bill McVeigh and his wide circle of friends—from his union, the American Legion hall, the church, the bowling league—can be invisible to the outside world. They are the solid, steady ones, the ones you can count on during a snowstorm to come jumpstart your car. They are barely recognized, much less celebrated, for their faithful work, their unselfish spirits. They are not the powerful, by the world's standards. They are the meek, the ones Jesus called blessed.

Timothy McVeigh must have looked over the quiet fields of Pendleton, his father's one-story house, the people at the fire company fundraiser, and thought, *I have to get out of here.*

And so he did.

On May 24, 1988, he drove to the army recruiting center in Lockport, a nondescript brick building near the locks in the heart of the city. He joined up and announced the fact to his father the day before he was to depart.

Both Bud and Bill blame the war for the drastic change in Timothy McVeigh, from unremarkable boy to the man he became, clenched with rage. It was the war that led Tim to the two virulent anti-government fanatics within the ranks of the army who would one day help him with the bomb plot: Michael Fortier and Terry Nichols.

Tim, Fortier, and Nichols had all enlisted in the army on the same day, in three different places. All three were sent to Fort Benning, Georgia, for basic training. They were part of a unit meant to create strong bonds among the soldiers by keeping them together from basic training throughout their service during their enlistment. All three were sent to Fort Riley for more training. McVeigh and Nichols went off for duty in the Persian Gulf, while a back problem kept Fortier behind in the US.

Nichols, who grew up on a farm in the "thumb" area of eastern Michigan, was a survivalist and gun enthusiast whose car was covered with pro-gun and anti-government bumper stickers. His hatred for government was so intense that he once cut up his driver's license, voter registration, and passport. Twice, Nichols attempted to renounce his US citizenship.

Fortier came from Kingman, Arizona, a working-class, Route 66 town and home to more than its share of anti-government militias and gun-rights absolutists. Drawn by lax weapons laws and open desert spaces in which to practice shooting and setting off explosives, paramilitary groups sprouted up in and around Kingman, plotting, at various times, to blow up power plants, government buildings, even the Hoover Dam.

"Meeting Nichols and Fortier were probably the

worst things that ever happened to him," Bill said. "Timmy never swore at Janet Reno and Bill Clinton on the TV before them."

Bud also attributes the change in Tim to psychological battle wounds. "McVeigh was telling neighbors the things he had seen in the war. He said he'd seen mine-sweepers bury Iraqi soldiers alive trying to surrender. He said he saw Iraqi soldiers running and American soldiers shooting them in the back. He and Nichols came back with PTSD. McVeigh had it the worst," Bud said.

In Iraq, Tim excelled in combat as a gunner on a Bradley assault vehicle but was traumatized by some of the atrocities he witnessed there. When he returned to the US, he tried out for an elite army unit. He quit after two days. "He wanted to be Special Forces, but he wasn't in shape enough," Bill said.

Tim grew frustrated and disillusioned with the army. In 1991, Tim left the service and moved back to Bill's house in Pendleton.

In the struggling economy of western New York, the best Tim could do was to get a low-paying job as a security guard. It was a jarring fall from his former height as a decorated soldier. Author Pankaj Mishra put it succinctly in his book *Age of Anger*: "McVeigh found it hard to get jobs commensurate with his sense of dignity."

Tim started writing angry letters to the newspaper, asking whether civil war was imminent and whether bloodshed was necessary to bring about change. He immersed himself in a racist, anti-Semitic novel, *The*

Turner Diaries, a story of a popular revolt against a tyrannical government featuring a truck bomb attack on the FBI. He yelled at the TV whenever Janet Reno, the US attorney general, came on.

When federal agents killed the wife and son of the white separatist Randy Weaver during a shootout near his cabin at Ruby Ridge, Idaho, in 1992, it only hardened Tim's view of the federal government as an enemy of its own people.

Tim started getting restless; he told Bill he was leaving New York, though Tim couldn't say where he was going. He ended up traveling to forty different US states, drifting about, making a living at short-term jobs and selling weapons at gun shows. Bill always knew he could reach his son by calling Nichols or Fortier.

In early 1993, during the federal government's fifty-one-day standoff over illegal weapons with cult leader David Koresh and his Branch Davidian followers, Tim went so far as to drive to the site of the compound, near Waco, Texas. He parked at a roadside spot nicknamed Fool's Hill, where hangers-on like him were allowed to gather. There, amid T-shirt vendors, psychics, singers, and protestors, Timothy McVeigh sat leaning against his car handing out anti-government pamphlets. He gave interviews to the press about his opposition to the Bureau of Alcohol, Tobacco, and Firearms (ATF) leading the siege.

Bill was baffled by what his son was doing. "Why would you sit on your car in Waco?" Bill asked. "What good's that going to do?"

Tim was visiting the Michigan home of Terry Nichols on April 19, 1993, when the images came on television: the Branch Davidian complex Tim had come so near to was engulfed in flames. The ATF had launched a tear gas attack on the compound—something that McVeigh, having experienced the excruciating effects of tear gas in the army, found unconscionable. The wooden complex started to collapse. Koresh's followers inside exchanged gunfire with federal agents outside. Dozens of Davidians died in the conflagration, from falling debris, injuries from the fire, and gunshot wounds.

When it was all over and federal agents had raised a flag over the smoking wreckage, the body count was shockingly high: seventy-six people were dead, including women and children.

Timothy McVeigh was incensed. Something had to be done.

Tim went to Michael Fortier's home, in Kingman, Arizona, where he would end up coming and going for months. There, Timothy McVeigh told Fortier he had a plan: to blow up a federal building.

PART 2 | Tragedy

CHAPTER 6

PLANNING

Timothy McVeigh's plan was crude but ingenious: he would turn a truck into a bomb.

His target would be a US government building, where his victims would include employees of the agencies he despised. The date he had chosen for the attack: April 19, the anniversary of the US government raid on the Branch Davidians in Waco. The date happened to fall on the two hundred twentieth anniversary of the Battles of Lexington and Concord, the shot heard round the world—the war for independence by revolutionaries against a vast, powerful government.

He picked the Alfred P. Murrah Federal Building in Oklahoma City after careful research. He looked into alternatives—buildings in Arkansas (home state of then president Clinton), Missouri, Arizona, and Texas. He even took another trip to Waco to check out the federal building there.

Waco was a more remote and dusty place then, before

it was transformed by Chip and Joanna Gaines and their hit TV show *Fixer Upper*. The potential target sat next to abandoned buildings and across from the glum exterior of Wally's bar. The building fell short of McVeigh's grandiose ambitions, according to Robert Darden, a Baylor journalism professor, historian, Waco resident, and author of many books, including one on the Branch Davidian conflagration, *Mad Man in Waco*. The federal building in Waco was a former post office that housed some courtrooms and a few offices rarely visited by the larger public. The body count would have been low; the employees killed would not have come from agencies responsible for the deadly raid on the Davidians' Waco compound. "If you've been thinking this through, and you want to make this grand gesture, one that would get you worldwide attention, Waco would have been a miserable spot," Darden said.

The Murrah building, by contrast, was ideal for McVeigh's purposes. The nine-story, thirteen-million-dollar structure contained offices of some of the federal agencies involved in Waco. The building had a glass front that would break easily, killing more people inside and giving McVeigh the high body count he wanted. He also wanted publicity; the big outdoor lot where Julie parked her car each day would provide open space around the building for television cameras to capture the devastation.

Timothy McVeigh was equipped to carry out his plan. He knew how to kill people; he had learned in the US Army. His killing of Iraqi soldiers in combat in Desert

Storm helped earn him one of the five medals bestowed on him by the army for his service.

He had experience in making and detonating explosives. Long before the Oklahoma City attack, McVeigh had started buying elements to build a bomb. He had practiced in the sunbaked desert outside Fortier's home in Kingman, Arizona, pouring the ingredients into a plastic Gatorade bottle and setting it off. His bomb worked.

McVeigh designed the bomb destined for Oklahoma City to kill as efficiently and effectively as possible. He decided on using fifty-five-gallon drums in place of the Gatorade bottle, and he arranged soup cans to experiment with the configuration of the drums. McVeigh set up the cans in different formations till he found the one that would cause the bomb to explode toward the building rather than away from it.

Once McVeigh settled on his plan, he needed help carrying it out. He got it, at times reluctantly, from his two army buddies: Michael Fortier and Terry Nichols.

Nichols and McVeigh had served in the Gulf War together, in the heat and dust and waking nightmare of battle. They experienced the same dislocation coming home to a society that counted their service as qualifying them for little more than low-paying, entry-level jobs. But all three former soldiers shared the same hostility toward a common enemy: the federal government.

Fortier was a survivalist who opposed any kind of gun regulation by the government he mistrusted. He flew a "Don't Tread on Me" flag, bearing a picture of a snake about to strike, outside his mobile home. Nichols went farther, rejecting the jurisdiction of any American court over him.

Timothy McVeigh figured both men had ways they could help him. Nichols grew up on a farm and had learned from his father how to blow up tree stumps by mixing fuel and fertilizer. Fortier could assist with some of the logistics of the plan, including inspecting the targeted structure to find its weakest point.

In late December 1994, Tim asked Fortier to drive with him from Arizona to Kansas on a mission to get some guns to sell. Tim wanted to stop on the way in Oklahoma City to case the Murrah building.

The two men drove slowly around the streets of Oklahoma City, which were lit with holiday lights. They surveyed the exterior of the Murrah building to find the best place to park the truck before setting off the bomb. They crossed the back of the building off the list of possibilities because elevator shafts fortified the rear. McVeigh and Fortier looked for a place nearby to stash a getaway car. Tim wanted to leave one close to the building, to escape in after the explosion. Then the two men slipped out of town as quietly as they had come, undetected.

Meanwhile, in the same quiet city, twenty-three-year-old Julie Marie Welch had some plans of her own.

Julie had decided to leave her job as an interpreter at the Social Security Administration on the first floor of the Murrah building. Her bosses and coworkers liked her, and she liked them. Her days were spent helping people who needed help, something that seemed hardwired into her system. But Julie was pursuing her dream job: teaching Spanish.

She landed a teaching job that would begin after the upcoming summer. Julie had put in applications for a number of positions; after her death, other schools she had applied to, not knowing she had perished in the bombing, called to offer her a teaching post.

Julie was looking ahead in her personal life too, contemplating a future with her boyfriend, Eric Hilz. They had met in August 1994 at a weekly young adult prayer meeting. It was held at Tinker Air Force Base, the military installation where Bill eight months later would fly into when the FBI took him to Oklahoma City for questioning. The base had a typically Oklahoman history of creation and destruction. It had been slammed by two massive tornadoes in 1948 that wiped out millions of dollars' worth of planes; it was also the site where Buddy Holly recorded the hit songs "Rock Me My Baby" and "You've Got Love" at the Officer's Club in 1957.

Eric was a young lieutenant who had been stationed at the base since May 1994. A strong Catholic, he had been attending the weekly prayer group at its Friday night meetings. Eric had just returned from a temporary duty assignment in Pennsylvania when he noticed a young woman he had never seen before, a pretty brunette, across the crowded room. She had sparkling blue eyes and a sweet smile.

Drawn instantly, the young airman didn't see Julie again for about a month, but she lingered in his mind.

Eric found Julie's combination of beauty and faith irresistibly attractive. "I couldn't wait to ask her out," Eric said in a remembrance.

His chance came on a night in late September 1994. The prayer group had just finished, and the young participants had moved out into the hallway to talk. When Julie started to leave, Eric followed her outside. "She threw a little smile over her shoulder at me, a smile meaning 'What are you doing?' more than 'Hi there,'" Eric remembered. He asked her where she lived and stammered when she returned the question, but he succeeded in getting her phone number. She got his too.

Their first date was in October 1994, dinner followed by a trip to the Oklahoma State Fair. She and Eric strolled the crowded midway, surrounded by the swirling lights of the Tilt-a-Whirl, the mustardy aroma of corn dogs, the happy chatter of preteens at the arcades, buoyant in their freedom to roam. The couple rode the Ferris wheel together, Julie airborne and radiant as the car lifted them skyward.

Romantic as it was, they did not kiss that night, instead building what Eric called "the key to any successful relationship—a solid friendship." Their first kiss came on Thanksgiving weekend. The following months pulled them closer.

Eric saw the messy parts of Julie—when she'd get annoyed with people who went on too long in church—and the funny, playful ones. Once, when they were clearing up breakfast dishes at her place, tango music came on the radio. Eric scooped her into his arms and the two began to dance a breathless, silly-serious tango around her living room. When the music stopped, they kept each other from falling over in laughter by standing there hugging. "That moment was the epitome of our time together," Eric said later. "It was joyous. It was innocent. It was supportive."

He saw the scrappy side of her too, the one Bud had known about from her first moments of life as a one-and-a-half-pound baby fighting to breathe. "Julie was not timid," Eric observed. "She was not afraid to give her opinion about something. On the other hand, she was just as open to listening as she was to expressing. She was tender and sweet, but also very strong-willed."

There is something about the word *intended*—a word from a former time to describe someone you love deeply, someone you mean to marry one day, whose future is the map of your own. *This man, this woman, this person, is my intended.* It carries with it hopefulness and purpose and dreams of a common destiny.

Eric wanted to propose to Julie someday in her beloved language of Spanish. She never got the chance to hear those words. Their planning was to be cut short soon. The time they had left together was ticking down.

Easter Sunday, April 16, 1995, Three Days Before

Many of the facts in the timeline that follows come with permission from the exceptional work of two reporters for *The Buffalo News*, Lou Michel and Dan Herbeck, and their book, *American Terrorist: Timothy McVeigh and the Oklahoma City Bombing* (Harper, 2001).

On a placid Sunday, when the people of predominantly Christian Oklahoma City were going to church for Easter services, Tim was heading to the city to stash his getaway car. He had the help of Terry Nichols, who by this time had moved to central Kansas to work as a ranch hand. The two army buddies met at a pizza shop near Nichols' home. Tim drove his beat-up Mercury Grand Marquis five hours to Oklahoma City, while Nichols followed in his truck.

Tim parked his car a few blocks from the Murrah building in a lot near a vacant house. He took his license plate off the back of the car, then parked close enough to some bushes to hide the empty spot where the plate was missing. He hopped into Nichols' truck, and the two men drove back to Kansas. Tim stayed the night in a motel.

While Tim was on the road, Julie was spending Easter Sunday with Eric and her mother, Lena, in Lena's hometown of Muskogee, Oklahoma. They visited the gardens at Honor Heights Park, known for its thousands of azaleas. The young couple walked through the park's rose garden, past the ponds, by a playground thronged by children. Eric snapped photo after photo of Julie, glorious amid the colors of the flowers.

Julie spent that night with her grandmother Ruby Mae Compassi, in the home where Julie's mother had grown up. Ruby Mae was a native Oklahoman who got her Italian last name from Julie's grandfather, an immigrant who had been studying for the priesthood before he left Italy for the US. She and Julie were close, spending almost every holiday together. Ruby Mae called her diminutive granddaughter "little ole gal," her ray of sunshine. Before bed, Julie asked her, "Grandma, how do you like my boyfriend?"

Monday, April 17, 1995, Two Days Before

Tim took a cab from his motel to a McDonald's near Elliott's Body Shop, a truck rental place in Junction City, Kansas. Tim walked over and, using the alias of Robert D. Kling, picked up a twenty-foot Ryder truck with a Florida plate. He showed the rental agent a fake ID that Michael Fortier's wife had helped him make using her clothes iron to laminate the plastic.

Safely in the truck, Tim drove to the Dreamland Motel in Junction City to spend the night. The motel's neon marquee was cinematic, something out of a Sam Shepard movie: the bright red outline of a star with the word "Dreamland" emblazoned in red and white lights inside, and the word "Welcome" in smaller block letters underneath. The motel has since been razed, by vote of the town's council. No one wanted this place where Timothy McVeigh dreamed of killing to become a mecca of hate.

He laid out his clothes for the next day and set his alarm for 4:00 a.m.

That same Monday, Julie was taking the day off work to plan Eric's twenty-fourth birthday celebration that night. She dropped by Bud's Texaco station to ask his advice: Where should she take Eric for dinner? "She wanted everything to be perfect," Bud recalled.

Bud told her to take him to Jamil's, a decades-old mainstay in a converted house on Lincoln Boulevard in Oklahoma City. The menu was exotic: tabouli, hummus, relish tray, Rose's cabbage rolls, and smoked bologna. The walls were deep red; gold chandeliers hung over the cozy tables. Paintings of local celebrities like former University of Oklahoma football coach Barry Switzer covered the walls.

Bud phoned and made reservations for the couple for that night. Still, Julie hung around the gas station for two hours, talking with him in between customers. Surrounded by the ordinary—the heavy sweet smell of gasoline, the ding of the bell when cars pulled up—father and daughter shared a moment that, even in the midst of it, felt extraordinary.

"When she came by, she never stayed that long," Bud told me. "When she walked to her car to leave, she hugged me the tightest and held me the longest she'd ever done before."

After that hug, Julie walked toward her car, a 1992 red Pontiac Grand Am that Bud had bought for her used. When she reached it, she turned and called out to Bud,

"I love you!" Julie ducked into the front seat, pulled the door shut, and drove away, disappearing into the traffic on 39th Street.

Those were the last words he heard his daughter say. It was the last time Bud ever saw her alive.

Tuesday, April 18, 1995, the Day Before

Tim woke on his own just before his alarm went off at 4:00 a.m.; it was a skill he had picked up in the army. He dressed and headed out the door by 4:30 a.m., slipping out into the darkness to the Ryder truck parked under the bright Dreamland sign.

He drove the truck twenty-five miles south to a storage unit in the town where Terry Nichols lived, Herington, Kansas. He and Nichols met there and loaded bomb-making supplies into the truck. Tim drove north, with Nichols following in his pickup, to nearby Geary Lake, a deep clear lake visited mostly by fishers. McVeigh and Nichols picked a remote spot, wanting to stay well away from other people as they began their deadly work.

At about 7:30 a.m., they started mixing the ingredients for the bomb. They poured the mixture into the fifty-five-gallon drums. It was slow, smelly, sweaty work; with the ingredients inside, each barrel weighed almost five hundred pounds. Tim arranged them into the configuration he had planned, with more barrels on the side closest to the target.

Then he did the painstaking work of setting up two fuses to ignite the bomb, one that would burn in two minutes, and a second, backup fuse that would burn in five. He connected both to blasting caps in the cargo bay. He would use an ordinary cigarette lighter to light them.

He wiped down the inside of the truck for fingerprints. He changed clothes and put on gloves, then parted ways with Nichols, heading south alone across the Kansas state line into Oklahoma.

That Tuesday, Julie was at work. When she got off at 5:00 p.m., she set off to meet her mother, Lena, at the 5:30 p.m. Mass at Little Flower Church. Little Flower was an old, burgundy brick church set on a stretch of busy street leading right into Oklahoma City's downtown. From the churchyard, bordered by a cyclone fence, you can see the city's steel and glass towers looming against the horizon.

Mass was said in Spanish, which drew Julie to the church. Much of its vibrant congregation had come from Mexico. Julie had just started volunteering at the church, playing with preschool-aged children who had just arrived and spoke little English. Those children, who had already left behind the life they knew in their home country, were soon to lose their kind and playful teacher.

Julie and Lena had dinner together after Mass. "Our time that week was so beautiful," Julie's mother recalled later. "It's as if, one by one, she was able to say goodbye to everybody she loved."

As Julie and her mother were getting ready for bed that night, Timothy McVeigh was pulling into an unpaved lot by a small motel. He turned off the truck and slept inside. His resting place that night was the very object he planned to use the next day to kill more people in a single incident than any other act of domestic terrorism in US history.

I imagine him closing his eyes that night, and wonder: Did he dream of them, the people who would walk innocently into that building the next day?

Scott Williams, the twenty-four-year-old salesperson for a food wholesaling company who happened to be making a delivery to the day care. The young husband was to become a father for the first time soon; the daughter he had already named, Kylie, was born three months to the day after he died in the bombing.

Peola Battle, 51, who loved to sew. She and her husband, Calvin, 62, were visiting the Social Security Administration office where Julie worked, planning the next stage of their lives when they died together.

Christy Rosas, 22, receptionist in the Federal Employees Credit Union office, who would leave behind a son she longed to see grow into manhood. After her death, the child wrote this note to her, in black magic marker on purple construction paper:

Dear Mom,

I miss you a lot. Life is sad without you. I'm growing like a weed and doing good in school. We all love you and miss you a lot.

Love,
Shane

Could Timothy McVeigh even comprehend the dreams of Anthony Christopher Cooper II—a big name for such a tiny child—who perished in the day care center along with his mother, Dana, who worked there? The toddler's favorite toy was a pink plastic Piglet, the cherished storybook character sitting atop a small blue-and-green globe. In the clear case in the Oklahoma City Memorial museum that commemorates Anthony's brief life, Piglet is smiling upward, his arms spread exuberantly to the sky. The little boy's future was as wide as that reach, an unlimited possibility.

What of Airman First Class Cartney J. McRaven, 19, who had married Senior Airman Shane McRaven only four days before the bombing? She had just returned from a four-month deployment to Haiti. Cartney had gone to the Social Security office to report her name change.

Did McVeigh give any thought to Robbin Ann Huff, 37, a loan officer in the credit union office? She went to bed that night feeling in her belly the tiny tugs of the baby in her womb, a little girl thirty-two weeks old she had not yet seen but had already given a name: Amber Denise.

Robbin Huff's dreams pierce my heart, because I can imagine what they must have been: like those of my sister Nancy, who was three months pregnant when bullets ripped through her, killing both her and her child.

Those dreams were simple, but to Nancy, they were everything: to hold her baby, warm in her arms, to kiss the fuzzy softness of its head. To lay her little one down to sleep, smelling of soap and cotton pajamas. Nancy had already started making those dreams concrete. When my family packed away her belongings after her murder, they found plastic baby bottles, tiny socks, a baby Christmas stocking Nancy had begun to needlepoint.

We know the stark, chilling truth: Timothy McVeigh thought of his victims not at all, except as "collateral damage," to use his own callous term. Their dreams and plans meant nothing to him. The people themselves were mere targets to him, like objects in the scope of a rifle.

As he drew closer to Oklahoma City, they did not know they were in his sights.

Wednesday, April 19, 1995

It was a perfect Oklahoma spring day: clear blue sky, calm winds—the kind of day you wear short sleeves and roll your car windows down on the way to work.

Ducks circled gently in the pond of Casady School, tiny ducklings trailing behind them. Branches of the weeping willow trees in Stars and Stripes Park drifted in the soft breeze. Runners bobbed along Lake Hefner, striding in peaceful rhythms on the sunlit pavement.

Politicians and businesspeople who had just finished their coffee emerged from the downtown convention center, where the mayor's annual prayer breakfast had ended at 8:30 a.m.

A steady stream of parents walked in bright sunshine to the Alfred P. Murrah Federal Building on their morning routine: dropping off their children at the America's Kids day care center on the second floor.

Julie was especially happy when she left home that morning, her mother remembered, because she had a scheduled meeting with a Spanish-speaking client at the Social Security office that day. Lena was on the phone with her own mother as Julie was on her way out the door. "I love you, Mom. Tell Grandma I love her," Julie said.

"That's how I remember Julie," Lena said later. "Exactly that way. She looked so pretty that morning."

As Julie was heading to morning Mass, Timothy McVeigh was in the Ryder truck, pulling quietly out of the parking lot where he had spent the night before.

He was wearing the clothes he'd planned for the occasion: army boots, jeans, a white T-shirt he had bought at a gun show, and a shoulder holster carrying a semiautomatic .45-caliber Glock pistol, loaded with armor-piercing cop-killer bullets.

The front of his T-shirt bore a sketch of President Abraham Lincoln and the Latin words, *Sic Semper Tyrannis* ("Thus Always to Tyrants"), the words Lincoln's assassin had shouted when he murdered the president. On the back was a drawing of a tree whose branches dripped with blood and a quote by Thomas Jefferson: "The Tree of Liberty must be refreshed from time to time with the blood of patriots and tyrants."

Law professor Mark Osler observes how out of context this quote is when hijacked by anti-government extremists like McVeigh. The quote by Jefferson comes from a letter the former president wrote in 1787 to a congressman from New York. The paragraph from which the quote comes, in fact, helps to explain the near-insanity of Timothy McVeigh's worldview: "The people can not be all, and always, well informed. The part [of the people] which is wrong will be discontented in proportion to the importance of the facts they misconceive."

While Tim was piloting his truck toward Oklahoma City, Julie was entering the 7:00 a.m. Mass at St. Charles Borromeo Church. The large red brick church, on a sprawling campus with its adjoining Catholic school, sits in a neighborhood of well-tended houses. The thud of basketballs on driveways and the sound of children's voices can be heard from the church's front door.

The priest at St. Charles later remembered that Julie had been there at church that morning. He told Bud that he had seen a Julie that day who had seemed totally at peace with herself.

As Tim was starting to see the outline of downtown Oklahoma City come into view, Julie was kneeling in a pew in the church's sanctuary. The smoky scent of incense hung in the air. She bowed her head and murmured this prayer, surrounded by the hushed voices of the other faithful around her: "Lamb of God, you take away the sins of the world, have mercy on us. Lamb of God, you take away the sins of the world, have mercy on us. Lamb of God, you take away the sins of the world, grant us peace."

Julie had just left church and was driving to work as

Tim was navigating the truck loaded with deadly explosives toward downtown.

By the time Julie had parked near the pool of shade cast by the lone tree in the employee lot and settled into work, Tim was approaching the corner of N. Harvey Avenue and NW 5th Street where the Murrah building stood. At 8:56 a.m., a security camera in the Regency Tower apartments, one block west of the Murrah building on NW 5th Street, captured a grainy black-and-white image of the Ryder truck as it passed in front.

Inside, Julie and three other employees were straightening up a stockroom in the back of the office. Julie was working there just as Tim was steering the rental truck toward the north side of the building. He put in earplugs that he had brought to ward off hearing damage from the enormous blast he knew was soon to come.

Close to 9:00 a.m., Julie was called to the front of the Social Security office to meet Emilio Tapia, 50, a father of five, accompanied by Reverend Gilbert Martinez, the pastor of El Tabernaculo de Fe Church. Rev. Martinez, 35, was also a father of five, the youngest only ten days old. Tapia had an appointment to try to get a Social Security card but spoke only Spanish. Rev. Martinez came along to help.

Julie's coworkers started to go to the front with her. Their supervisor stopped them, asking them to stay in the stockroom and finish throwing out outdated forms. Julie had left the area about a minute and a half before the bomb went off. Her three fellow staffers in the stockroom survived. They were rescued forty-five minutes later.

"I'll never forget the look on her face as Julie said to me, 'I'll be back in a minute,' as she turned and walked away," one of those coworkers, Sara Reed, said later. "That image haunts me even now."

Julie Marie Welch, this young woman who loved her life, could not have known that the two minutes between 9:00 a.m. and 9:02 a.m. would mean annihilation instead of survival, that her dreams of teaching Spanish to a boisterous class of children, or of walking down an aisle toward her beloved Eric, would never be. She could not have known that she was going to her doom.

She greeted the man who needed her, and the pastor who came with him, at the front of her office. She started to walk with them toward the back.

Outside, Timothy McVeigh was ready for his moment.

He flipped his cigarette lighter and lit the fuses.

He pulled the truck into the loading spot closest to the building, parking just beneath the windows of the day care.

He stepped away from the truck as the fuses burned down. There was little time left, for little Anthony Cooper, for Emilio Rangel Tapia, for Peola and Calvin Battle, for Julie. The spark had almost met the charge.

Timothy McVeigh walked quickly across NW 6th Street, into the alley, to shield himself from the blast.

Then he ran.

CHAPTER 7

THE DAY

The little boy come home from play . . .
stares at us from the rubble
and tomb of his home,
his parents, his brother,
his life. He stares at us
forever. All her dangers, too
on our doorstep the moment after
some magician has pointed
his wand and, Poof!
Everything is gone.

—CAROL HAMILTON, Oklahoma's poet
laureate in 1995, from "Face of War"

Bud was at home. His wife's son Christopher was over. Suddenly, an enormous boom sounded outside.

Bud remembers, "Chris said, 'What was that?' I said, 'I don't know.' The house shook. Then we heard a second boom about three seconds later: it was all the debris blown in the air crashing back down."

Bud thought it could have been a plane crash; his house was on the approach path to Will Rogers World Airport in Oklahoma City.

Bud's brother Frank called from his car on a local expressway. "Do you have your television on?" he asked Bud. "There's a big fire downtown."

Bud turned the TV on and saw Channel 9's helicopter approaching from the north. "You could see the big plume of smoke and the whole north face of the building totally gone. When I saw that, my heart just sunk. I knew Julie worked on the first floor. The place where she worked was a three-story-high pile of rubble."

At 9:02 a.m., Timothy McVeigh's bomb had exploded on the north side of the building; that entire side of the building collapsed.

Twelve miles away, my childhood friend Dixie Hendrix was at her parents' house. When she heard the boom, they all went outside and saw smoke pouring into the sky from downtown. After the loud explosion, there was silence—the sirens had not started yet—but the neighbor's dog stood alert for ten minutes afterward, listening for something Dixie could not hear. She found out later what it was: the sound of glass breaking and crashing to the ground in buildings all over the city. The force of the blast cracked windows as far north as Guthrie, about thirty miles away.

The Official Record of the Oklahoma City Bombing, published by *Oklahoma Today* magazine, reported, "The first wave of super hot gas moved at 7,000 miles an hour, fast enough that someone ten feet away would have been hit with a force equal to thirty-seven tons. In about a half second, the gas dissipated, only to be replaced by an equally violent vacuum. The resulting pressure wave moved outward, lifting the building up and causing beams, floor slabs, and connections to weaken or collapse. When the pressure wave passed, gravity took over. Nine stories on the north side of the Alfred P. Murrah Federal Building pancaked, creating a crater some thirty feet deep."

An Oklahoma City dentist, who later volunteered in the effort to identify bodies by their dental records, said that all the faces of the dead looked like Edvard Munch's painting *The Scream,* with mouths wide open. A colleague told her, "What happens in a bomb, you get this huge blast and your lungs go [gasp sound] and that was the expression; they're frozen in their last expression."

Survivors of the blast recall seeing people across from them with their arms flung up in the air, as if they were doing the wave at a football game. They were falling through empty space; people who worked on the Murrah building's ninth floor were found at the base of the building, eight stories down. The force of the explosion drove some people through cinder block walls.

At the moment the bomb exploded, Bill had just gotten off work doing the night shift at the plant in Lockport, New York. He had headed home to get something to eat and some sleep. He knew nothing of the blast that had just sheared off the front of the Murrah building.

At the Oklahoma State Capitol, miles away from the building, Oklahoma governor Frank Keating was in his office. He had been on the job only a few months. Keating had just returned from the Oklahoma City prayer breakfast that morning when he heard a strange sound.

"The office had bulletproof glass. You could feel a 'whump whump' movement of the glass," Keating said. "I thought it was a munitions dump that had blown or a plane crash. I turned on the TV and saw a helicopter flying over the Murrah building and all the cars burning."

Someone in Keating's office said it might be a natural gas explosion, but with his long background in the FBI, Keating knew better. "I thought, that looks like somebody blew the place up—it was just so huge and violent." Within minutes, Keating got a phone call from President Bill Clinton, wanting to know what had happened and what he could do to help.

Keating sped to the scene. The air was bitter with smoke from fires that were still burning. Loose papers from offices in the building were blowing everywhere.

Bob Johnson, a lawyer who went on to become the founding chair of the Oklahoma City National Memorial and Museum, was in his office about five blocks away from the federal building. His office window looked out on a roofing crew working on a hotel across from his building. When he heard the blast, Johnson saw the crew duck and look north. Johnson at first thought it was a gas explosion. He and his law partners turned on a television. "A local television station happened to have a helicopter in the area, and video showed most of the north side of the building had been blown away. We were shocked—absolutely shocked."

Back at his home, Bud was fixed on the images on TV. "I could clearly see the front of the building was gone," Bud said. "I waited here at home, because I knew if Julie had gotten out, the first thing she would do is call me. I wanted to stay by the phone. I knew there was nothing I could do down there." Bud had no cell phone at the time. A phone company donated cell phones to all the families of people missing in the Murrah building three days later.

As Bud was waiting by the phone, his sisters and brothers started calling all the hospitals to see if Julie had been admitted. Julie's boyfriend, Eric, rushed to Bud's home. "He was just stunned," Bud recalled.

Calls to police and fire departments flooded in within minutes of the explosion. By 9:20 a.m., the first rescuers began to arrive. A short while later, for the first time in Oklahoma City's history, all on- and off-duty firefighters were called into service.

Rescuers frantically tried to evacuate those trapped

inside but still living. One woman pinned under a steel beam, Daina Bradley, had to have her right leg amputated without anesthetic to free her before she would have been crushed to death. The doctor had to use his own pocketknife to finish severing her limb when his other instruments gave out.

Florence Rogers had been in a meeting in her office at the credit union with eight of her employees, all women. "At 9:02 a.m., wham, they disappeared. All eight of 'em in my office. Just gone," Rogers said later. Rogers climbed onto an eighteen-inch ledge, all that remained of her office, then made it down a flight of stairs until someone carried her out. Of all the women in that meeting, she alone survived.

The scene was an unimagined hell: the tiny shoes of toddlers sticking out from under the wreckage of the building's day care center; people impaled on rebar, screaming as they bled to death; office workers clinging to a precipice that had once been a floor where a coworker had stood. Men whose shirts had been ripped open stumbled out, their backs red with blood. People emerged ghostlike, covered in grayish-white dust blanketing their skin and hair.

Randy Norfleet, a marine captain whose skull was fractured in the bombing, escaped the building by following a trail of blood left by other survivors. Luke Franey ran down a stairwell holding a handrail that was covered in blood.

People rushed in to help with rescue efforts. "One

doctor drove in from Muskogee with medical supplies and just treated people on the sidewalk. He didn't know what number [of people]," Bud said. Other victims, dazed and bloody, just walked away from the scene. "To this day, they don't know how many people had injuries."

First responders began to bring out bodies of the children. In the day care, fifteen were dead, ranging in age from six-month-old Antonio Ansara Cooper Jr. to five-year-old Aaron M. Coverdale, whose little brother Elijah S., age two, also died in the blast.

One man at Tim McVeigh's trial later described having to hold back parents as their children were laid on broken glass on the ground. Helena Garrett's frantic search for her tiny son led her to the line of dead bodies on the glass-covered street. She pleaded for workers not to lay the babies on the glass, not realizing they were already dead.

Boston Globe editorial cartoonist Dan Wasserman drew an image that afternoon that became a symbol of inexpressible grief over the slaughter of the children: a teddy bear with its head bowed and a paw covering its eyes as it wept.

Only six children from the day care were dug out from the ruins alive. The youngest of those, one-year-old Joseph Webber, was at the time the only child of Dan Webber, a law clerk who went on to become the lead federal prosecutor for the western district of Oklahoma.

Dan Webber was working at the federal courthouse, just south of the Murrah building, when the explosion hit. Webber escaped his damaged office and bolted across a plaza that led to the second-floor day care, where he had dropped off his child thirty minutes earlier. Webber arrived only to find that there was no longer a second floor—only a vast gray pile of ash.

After long, agonizing moments, a police officer pulled Joseph out. The toddler had a broken arm and jaw, two ruptured eardrums, and deep lacerations on his face, but he was alive. Webber later told the *Tulsa World* newspaper, "It's the feeling of having everything you care about being taken away from you and then given back."

Chris Fields was the first responder who appeared in the iconic photo shown around the world: a firefighter carrying the limp, bloody body of one-year-old Miss Baylee Almon. When the picture was taken, she was already dead. It was the day after her first birthday.

After handing the child's lifeless body over to paramedics, Fields returned to the recovery effort. He and other rescuers were able to dig out a twenty-eight-year-old woman, a newlywed who was three months pregnant. She was so covered with debris that they asked her to keep talking so they could find her. She told them her name: Sheila Driver. Later, Fields was overcome to see Driver's name on a list of the deceased; she had died on the way to the hospital.

Rescuers frantically tried to save others. Jon Hansen of the Oklahoma City Fire Department told the *New York Times* that there were places they had to crawl over bodies to get to other people who were still alive. He could hear the voices of people crying out to them and tried to reach through and touch their hands.

Canine search and rescue teams combed through huge piles of broken concrete, bent metal, coin purses, shoes, phones, office furniture, toys, and slivers of glass, trying to sniff out survivors. A dog would signal a "hit"—the scent of a human—raising hopes that someone would be pulled out alive. Those hopes were dashed when rescuers found only part of a body instead.

Though the search lasted for weeks, the last discovery of a person alive in the ruins of the building occurred the evening of that first day, the day of the explosion; rescuers pulled out a fifteen-year-old girl who had been visiting the Social Security office where Julie worked.

Doctors and nurses flocked to the bombing site and to hospitals to help with triage. One nurse, Rebecca Anderson, a thirty-seven-year-old mother of four who had come to treat victims, herself became one of the bombing's casualties when falling debris struck her head. She died of her injuries four days later; her organs were donated to transplant patients.

Rescue efforts became even more difficult as rain moved into the area and forty-five-mile-per-hour winds swept through the shattered building. As it grew dark, searchlights were brought in, casting a ghostly glow on the nightmarish ruins.

The site immediately became a crime scene. Investigators combing the area found a key piece of evidence: an axle from the blown-up Ryder truck bearing a vehicle identification number. The number was traced to a truck at the rental outlet in Junction City, Kansas, where, two days before, a sharp-featured white man with a crew cut had rented the truck under the name Robert Kling. Then another crucial piece of evidence was plucked from the wreckage: the rear bumper of that same rented truck, its license plate still attached.

At the same time, Bill McVeigh was working at the plant in Lockport, operating the furnace on the night shift. Later that day, the day of the bombing, Bill was watching the 6:00 p.m. news before he had to leave to run the bingo game at his church. Images of the wounded Murrah building floated across the screen. Bill listened to reports about the explosion and felt bad but didn't think much more about it.

He got to Good Shepherd Church by 7:30 that night to work the bingo. A few of the church ladies were talking about the disaster in Oklahoma City. Bill asked them what had happened; he imagined the structure going up from a gas leak. The women told him that it had been a deliberate attack and that the identity of the attacker was unknown.

At the same moment, I was stopping by to see my parents at their home in the Chicago suburbs. The news was on in the den where my dad would sit on an orange couch and smoke his pipe and watch TV. The screen showed a large office building whose front had been torn off, pouring smoke. The crawl at the bottom of the screen said something about an attack on Oklahoma City. My dad turned up the sound.

The horrors we were witnessing—bloody bodies being taken out of the shattered building—stood in stark contrast to the beauty of the morning there. In the initial images captured on broadcasts from Oklahoma City, the sun was shining; people were dressed in shirtsleeves. It was surreal.

We sat silently in front of the TV, stunned. Not since Pearl Harbor had there been as deadly a strike on American soil.

I spent the rest of the evening calling to check on loved ones there: my aunt and uncle, high school classmates, church friends, former neighbors. They all were okay, physically. But their shock was palpable. No one had seen this coming, this purposeful act of hate.

Bud went to bed that night in Oklahoma City not knowing for certain where his daughter was, how injured she was, or whether she was even alive.

When I try to imagine that, I think of my dad and the murder of his youngest daughter. On the day my father found my sister Nancy and her husband, Richard, slain in their townhouse, after police had processed the crime scene, Nancy's body was taken to the Cook County morgue and laid on a cold slab.

Her body was evidence. Police needed to do fingernail scrapings, searches for fibers or DNA that might provide a clue to the identity of whoever had killed her.

My father could not bear it. That was his baby lying there, alone in the cold dark. When, after several days, police and prosecutors still resisted releasing her body so that she could be cremated and buried safely in the earth, my father called me in frustration. I begged him to be patient.

I began to grasp how hard it was for him, finally, on the day of Nancy's funeral. The small box cradling her ashes was to be laid in the memorial garden outside Kenilworth Union Church, where she and Richard had been married only a few years before. Nancy's ashes had been placed by the open grave but not yet buried when the signal came for everyone to go inside for the memorial service to begin.

My father would not budge. I implored him to come into the church. He looked at me steadily and told me his creed, sprung from his deep roots growing up on an Illinois farm: you don't leave till the last spade of earth is turned. He would not leave his daughter alone and unburied.

Bud, raised on a farm like my dad, must have known that creed in the core of his being. As he turned out the lights that night, Bud felt the agony of how alone and unguarded his daughter, Julie, was, wherever she was. Bud went to bed in Oklahoma City that night, but he did not sleep.

Far away, in Pendleton, Bill lay down for what would be one of the last peaceful sleeps he would have for a very long time. He did not know that the intense manhunt for his son was in motion.

Bud's heartache had just begun. Bill's was soon to come.

CHAPTER 8

THE AFTERMATH

The day after the bombing, Thursday, Bud and his wife, Lois, drove toward the site but couldn't get near it. Police had blocked off the streets.

"The building was on 5th Street, and the closest you could get was 9th Street. You could park your car and walk to 7th Street. There were more barricades there; they wouldn't let people get any closer," Bud remembered. "I told the officer, 'My daughter's in the building,' and he let me go a block closer, but still not close enough to see the building."

Governor Keating and his wife, Cathy, had already been to the building together early that morning, around 6:00 a.m. "You didn't hear anything. It was just deathly quiet," Keating said.

"By then, big light trucks were shining lights on everything. A firefighter came up, not wearing an Oklahoma uniform, from somewhere else. I stepped out and said, 'Thank you for being here.' He said, 'Who are you?' I said, 'I'm the governor.' He didn't say nice to meet you, etc. He punched his finger in my chest and said, 'Well, you find out who did this, because the only thing I pulled from the rubble was a child's finger and the American flag.'"

One team leader supervising rescue workers doing twelve-hour shifts said he was having a hard time getting them to take a break.

Huge refrigerated trucks were parked nearby to receive the bodies, and body parts, of victims. Rescue dogs were so despondent over finding no survivors that first responders took turns hiding in the debris of the destroyed building, to give the dogs the reward of finding a living human and not a corpse.

People lined up to donate blood, from Hells Angels to businesspeople in suits, in lines so long it often took six or seven hours to give. Members of the Oklahoma Restaurant Association started a twenty-four-hour food service for rescue workers, serving up to twenty thousand meals per day for the next ten days.

Press from around the globe descended on Oklahoma City. Getting there was rough; storms had rolled in, with lightning strikes all around the airport. One journalist reported flying in on a plane whose approach at Will Rogers World Airport was so bumpy that passengers were throwing up. When reporters arrived at the scene of the bombing, they fared not much better; one remembered being overwhelmed by the stench of dead flesh rotting in the rain.

The catastrophe dominated national and world news for days on end. The coverage was stunned and sympathetic. One journalist, George Howe Colt for *Life* magazine, wrote, "To the millions of Americans who watched body after body being borne from the wreckage—some of them so small that weeping firefighters couldn't bear to look down at what they so gently cradled—it seemed as if the heart of the nation itself had been sundered."

Desperate for news of Julie, Bud went to First Christian Church to sign up for notifications. A family assistance center was created at the downtown church within hours after the bombing as a place where families could get news of their loved ones' fates. Bud gave Julie's name and identifying information. The place was crowded with anxious family members, Red Cross volunteers, clergy, counselors, and—least wanted—funeral directors.

Within days, my friend Dixie, who had joined me all those years ago playing hooky from Sunday school, was asked to volunteer at the center. She had become a child psychologist and mother of a two-year-old boy. "In the first two days after the bombing, everybody was glued to the TV," she told me. "There were all these alerts coming. Like the paws of rescue dogs that had come in from all over the country were getting hurt by the broken glass, so people sent in thousands of dog booties. The entire community was focused on what was needed and was trying to help."

Though it was called a family reunification center, Dixie added, by this time, nobody would be reunified with any living survivor of the blast. "Everyone was dead, but no one knew it."

Dixie downplayed her status as a psychologist, saying, "It wasn't really psychology, it was just being human. The people who came thinking, 'They need therapy,' were off the mark. It wasn't therapy; it was just being kind. The families didn't need fixing. They needed their family members. They needed to know."

Dixie's role was not so much counselor as concierge, somebody to get families things they needed or to be a go-between with unwanted intruders.

One family wanted Dixie to ask a pastor who was there to leave them alone. The clergyman wanted to pray with the family, and they didn't want that; they just wanted information about their loved one. Dixie approached and politely asked him to go because he was making the family uncomfortable. He replied, "I'm just praying with them!" She answered, "That's what's making them uncomfortable." He left.

Other clergy were part of teams of volunteers whose jobs were to notify waiting families that their loved ones had been found.

Roger Paynter, a Baptist minister and pastoral counselor, was one of those clergy volunteers. He had grown up in Oklahoma City with another volunteer, Randy Aschcraft. The two men had played football together at Putnam City, a large public high school that Dixie had also attended.

At the time of the bombing, Paynter was forty-five years old and pastor of a church in Jackson, Mississippi. He and Aschcraft had gone fly fishing, staying at a cabin owned by a church member. "We turned on the TV, and there was the news," Paynter told me. "We were absolutely in shock. Just total disbelief.

"We called a pastor friend of ours, up in far northwest Oklahoma City; he had heard the rumble and felt the shock. He was describing to us the chaos. We both said, we need to get there—we need to go home."

Paynter and his friend got there the next day and went to the gathering area at First Christian Church. They were told to come back the following day. The church was chaos, packed with family members and officials. People wore ribbons to color-code what role they played.

"The church had just turned the entire building over to this effort. They made every room available: places for families, for eating, for firemen to come and rest," Paynter said.

Paynter and his friend got as close as they could to the Murrah building. They weren't allowed to get nearer than three blocks away. The building was still smoking. "We were both just sick to our stomachs," Paynter recalled.

The two pastors stayed in Oklahoma City for almost three weeks, first undergoing a training session. They each were assigned to a team with a psychiatrist, a medical doctor, a social worker, and either Roger or Randy as chaplain. Their job: death notifications.

"We would meet with the families of the victims," Paynter recalled. "At this point, they were beginning to make IDs of the bodies. We would have to meet with the families and tell them their loved one had been found."

It did not always go well.

"The very first family I dealt with, it just blew up," Paynter said. The father of a daughter who died in the bombing, like Bud, "was just broken by it. He couldn't contain his rage. I've counseled people who have been that angry. Before then, I would say I was afraid of anger. Try to calm people down, back up from it. I think here there's a sense in which the explosion of anger itself just had to be. There wasn't any stopping it, there wasn't any talking him down. How close can you stand to the fire?"

Paynter's second death notification, that same day, was "the exact opposite" of the first, he remembered. A family had lost a young man who had worked as an accountant in the building but was hoping to join the FBI.

"They were so terribly grieved, but so grateful also that we were meeting with them to answer questions, that we cared. They just had lots of questions: Was the body broken apart? Where exactly did he fall? Could you tell if he died immediately? How did he die—from the explosion, or from something falling on him?

"The first one, there had been so much rage in the room—you could kind of understand the rage, and the whole thing sparked some in myself," Paynter said. "But this was a really sweet family. They were just heartbroken.

They had so many hopes for him, and it just came out of the blue. I prayed, and each one of them prayed: 'He is in heaven, he is okay, God can repair his body.' That it made no sense seemed to bother them less than it did the first family."

Paynter worked with one family where all that was found of their loved one was a finger, identified from a fingerprint. "In some ways, I think it was harder," Paynter said, than if there had been no trace at all.

Every notification was different. Some of them were quiet. Always there were tears. Sometimes wailing, as one grandmother did when she heard the name of her infant grandchild spoken in a prayer for the dead. Sometimes there had been so many days that had gone by that the family already had lost all hope.

What remained of the Murrah building was in danger of falling down upon itself. The weather was warm but rainy; one day, the search for bodies was called off because of rain and wind. "The top of the building started to swing," Bud said. "They were afraid the building was going to collapse."

The Murrah building was one of many in Oklahoma City seriously injured by the bomb—but, strikingly, no scavengers came to pick through the remnants.

"We had three hundred and two downtown buildings damaged or destroyed, but not one act of looting," said Frank Keating, then governor of Oklahoma. "Every community has bad people who do bad things, but here, when the bombing occurred, crime just collapsed."

The vault of the Federal Employees Credit Union had been blown apart, sending thousands of dollars in cash floating into the streets below. People collected the money and returned it—adding up to a total greater than the amount lost. Downtown banks whose glass windows crashed to the ground were left standing open; their cash drawers were untouched.

The city united in embracing the volunteers who came to help. "Everything people needed—meals, laundry, bedding—was free of charge. You'd go out to dinner and the check never came," Keating said. "Teams of responders came from all over the country. One man, when he was leaving, held up a dollar bill and said, 'Hey, Governor, do you know what this is? This is an Oklahoma dollar. It's the dollar I brought with me, the same dollar I am leaving with.' He never got to spend it, because no one would take it."

Oklahoma's history of disasters—earthquakes, tornados, the Dust Bowl—had prepared them well. Many Oklahomans' ancestors had passed down stories of having helped rebuild a neighbor's barn when it burned down, or plow a field when a neighbor got sick or died.

"There's a special attribute that people in Oklahoma have, and I think it has to do with what we have all inherited as part of the pioneering era. And that is neighbor helping neighbor," Keating said.

Some volunteers from Michigan were wary of how they might be received in Oklahoma City, since bombing coconspirator Terry Nichols was from Michigan.

When the group was about to cross the state line into Oklahoma, it got word that Oklahoma state troopers were coming to meet them at the border to escort them in, a gesture of profound gratitude and respect.

A large contingent of firefighters from New York City arrived to help; later, some of them were killed in the terrorist attack on their own city on September 11, 2001.

On Friday, two days after the bombing, Bud waited for news of Julie, whose body still had not been reported found.

Meanwhile that day, Bill McVeigh was returning to his home in Pendleton at 11:30 a.m. from an overtime shift at work the night before. He picked up his morning newspaper and saw a sketch of the slender, sharp-featured white male with the buzz cut who was the suspect in the bombing. Bill peered at the picture and thought, *At least it's not Tim.*

An FBI artist had drawn the sketch from descriptions of the man who had rented the Ryder truck in Junction City, Kansas. The FBI combed that city with the sketch until they found someone who recognized him: the manager of the Dreamland Motel. She remembered the man who had checked out only days before, who had signed in under a different name: Timothy McVeigh.

Bill went to bed and was sleeping when the FBI rang about an hour later. "When they called, then it hit me," Bill told me. "I said to myself, maybe that picture was Tim."

Bill remembered the call as if it were yesterday: "'Mr. McVeigh, can we talk to you? It's the FBI. We want to talk to you.' I said sure. I said, give me a couple of minutes, I'm in bed. When I got up, they were in the driveway. I think they called from down at the corner. There was two of them in the car. One come to the door. I said come on in; he waved at the SWAT team of cars out front."

Bill recalled the Randy Weaver shootout not long before; he understood why the FBI agents would be wary.

Bill welcomed them in. "The FBI showed me the paper with the sketch on it and said, 'Is this your son?' I said I guess it could be, I didn't think it was when I looked at it this morning. And we went from there."

After FBI agents had been at Bill's talking for about an hour, they got a call: their suspect had been caught. An Oklahoma state trooper had picked him up after a traffic stop and had taken him to the Noble County Jail in Perry, Oklahoma, a small town of 5,340 people. The man in custody was Bill's son, Tim. "It was like a shock," Bill recalled.

Only seventy-seven minutes after the explosion, Oklahoma State Trooper Charles Hanger had noticed a 1977 yellow Mercury Marquis driving with no license tags. Behind the wheel, Timothy McVeigh was heading northbound from Oklahoma City toward Kansas on I-35. The trooper pulled him over just before the exit for Billings, Oklahoma, seventy-seven miles north of the Murrah building.

When McVeigh revealed that he had a concealed,

loaded gun, the trooper placed him under arrest. Timothy McVeigh was charged with four misdemeanors: unlawfully carrying a weapon, transporting a loaded firearm in a motor vehicle, failure to display a current license plate, and no proof of insurance.

Trooper Hanger took Tim to the Noble County Jail and booked him on the four charges. The jailer took Tim's clothes and property and issued him an orange jail uniform. Timothy McVeigh was caught—and would have been let go soon but for a fluke.

Tim was held there for two days, awaiting a bond hearing before a county judge. On the first day, Thursday, April 20, the judge's schedule was too busy to hold one. The second day, Friday, April 21, the normal court schedule changed because the judge's son had missed his school bus that morning. Tim was almost ready to enter the Noble County courtroom for the hearing that likely would have freed him, when he was suddenly called out and put back in his jail cell on the fourth floor of the same building. Something was up.

The FBI had been searching for Timothy McVeigh in a national database and found that, within hours of the bombing, that name had been run by Oklahoma State Trooper Charles Hanger in Perry, Oklahoma. A federal agent called the sheriff's office in Perry and got jaw-dropping news: Timothy McVeigh, the man they were looking for, was there in the Noble County Jail. The agent shouted, "Hold him!" and quickly ended the call.

Federal agents rushed to Noble County. They tested

Tim's clothes and earplugs and found them covered with explosives residue. An inventory search of Tim's getaway car revealed a sealed envelope with documents arguing that because the federal government had launched open warfare against Americans, killing government officials was a justified defense of liberty.

That same day, Friday, April 21, 1995, the federal government filed charges against Timothy McVeigh for unlawful destruction by explosives. Agents took Tim into federal custody. They prepared to transfer him from the small county jail where he was being held to a secure federal prison in El Reno, Oklahoma, a half-hour west of Oklahoma City.

The scene of federal agents leading Timothy McVeigh out of the Noble County Jail into daylight is an indelible image in American history: his orange jumpsuit; his buzz-cut wedge of hair; the narrow slits of his eyes, trying not to blink in the bright sun. People had gathered outside the jail when they learned that the suspect in one of the most horrific crimes in the nation's history was in their midst; they erupted in outraged shouts of "murderer" and "baby killer" when he was brought out.

Roger Paynter saw Timothy McVeigh's perp walk from Noble County Jail on television and flashed back to the prisoner transport of Lee Harvey Oswald, the man accused of assassinating President John F. Kennedy in Dallas in 1963. "When I was a kid growing up in Ardmore, Oklahoma, I was watching TV at home when they brought out Oswald and Jack Ruby shot him," Paynter said. "That is exactly what I thought of when I saw them taking McVeigh out of that building in the orange jumpsuit. I thought, that's a target. I guarantee you, he's not safe."

Bud, at home watching the images of Timothy McVeigh emerging into sunlight, had the same thought—and hoped it would come to pass. "I wished a sniper would take him out right there," Bud told me.

Reporters were in front of Bill's house in Pendleton within hours of the FBI's arrival. By Friday afternoon, state police had to block off the road from the swarm of news trucks and cameras.

"I stayed in," Bill said. "I had a state trooper in my yard for two weeks, guarding the house. I kept calm. I don't know how I did. I didn't talk to any of them for I don't know how long. After a while, I accepted it. They would wait at the door, in a line. I would talk to them one at a time, right up until the time he got executed."

The FBI searched the house, carried away Tim's belongings, tapped Bill's phone. FBI agents took Bill straight from his home to a hotel in Buffalo, where they stayed the night.

At 9:30 a.m. the next day, Saturday, April 22, they flew Bill out of Niagara Falls Air Reserve Station on a C-130 cargo plane to Tinker Air Force Base in Oklahoma City. Bill and two FBI agents sat on fold-down seats in the back.

When they landed at the base in Oklahoma City, the National Guard was there, on alert. "Five or six guys were walking back and forth with rifles," Bill remembered.

"They started talking about Timmy. They didn't know who I was. Every time they saw him on TV, they'd say, 'Oh, I'd do this and that to him.' One of the agents told them, 'Guys, you gotta be respectful. This is Timothy McVeigh's father here.' They went berserk—put me in a separate room."

FBI agents drove Bill into downtown Oklahoma City, where rescuers were still looking for bodies in the Murrah building. The FBI agents asked if Bill wanted to see it. Bill said no.

The agents questioned Bill for a couple of hours; Bill told them everything he knew.

At the same time, that Saturday, Bud had gone to First Christian Church for news of Julie. When he had signed up, he had put down Catholic for his family's religion. A priest was there to meet him. Bud got the heartbreaking news he had been expecting: Julie had been found, dead.

Bud guessed that her body had been located days earlier, but that he had not been notified till then. "The FBI had said on Wednesday evening that there would be a long time after bodies would be handed over to families. They wanted to test clothes and skin for explosives."

Along with Julie, a staggering total of five married couples had been killed in the first-floor Social Security Administration office where she worked. All of them were there to plan for a future they would never live to see.

Luther H. Treanor, 61, and LaRue A. Treanor,

55, parents of four and grandparents of one, a grand-daughter, Ashley Eckles. Luther had delivered milk for twenty-nine years. They lived in an 1800s farmhouse on 160 acres near Guthrie, Oklahoma, where they grazed three hundred head of cattle. Luther knew every one of his cows by sight. LaRue sang in her church choir and baked legendary cinnamon rolls. Four-year-old Ashley, who was spending the day with her grandparents, died with them.

Robert Lee Luster, 45, and Aurelia Donna Luster, 43, parents of six children. Bobby had been a maintenance man until he suffered a heart attack. Donna was a homemaker. A lover of Western novels, Bobby was known as a bighearted man who would give you his last nickel.

Dr. Charles E. Hurlburt, 73, and Jean Nutting Hurlburt, 67, parents of four daughters. They met at Wheaton College in Illinois, married, and spent five years as medical missionaries in Africa. Jean was a nurse, Charles a retired professor and director of dental radiology at OU Health Sciences Center. Both sang in their church choir at Metropolitan Baptist in Oklahoma City.

Don Fritzler, 64, and Mary Anne Fritzler, 57, parents of a daughter and a son. Don was an architect and Mary Anne a retired schoolteacher. They attended Quail Springs Baptist Church, which Don had designed and where Mary Anne taught Sunday school. They had learned only weeks before the bombing that their first grandchild was on the way.

Calvin Battle, 62, and Peola Battle, 51, parents of four. Calvin had worked as a machinist for thirty years until he had a stroke. The Battle residence was a constantly rotating constellation of visiting children and grandchildren. Peola, who worked as a process operator for a tech company, was an avid gardener and seamstress who made all the bridesmaid dresses for the wedding of one of her daughters.

On Saturday afternoon, Bud and his wife, Lois; Julie's mother, Lena; and Julie's boyfriend, Eric, went to view Julie at the mortuary. Her neck was broken. One side of her head was crushed in. Lacerations scarred her face. Both ankles were broken, with one foot almost severed. A scapular, a Catholic religious necklace, was around her neck. "There was tremendous trauma to the left side of her head. The report we got was she would have been killed instantly," Bud said.

Not until that moment had Bud come to terms with the fact that his daughter was really dead. "I'm not sure I completely accepted that until I saw her."

At the same time on Saturday, President Bill Clinton was speaking to a huge gathering of mourners at a memorial service at the Oklahoma State Fairgrounds Arena in Oklahoma City. My friend Dixie was there with her choral group, Canterbury Voices, to sing at the event. She sat only a short distance away from Clinton as he tried to console the grieving people of Oklahoma City.

President Clinton told the crowd he had met with

some children of the federal employees who worked in the building; one girl had suggested that everyone plant a tree in memory of the children who died there. Clinton said that a dogwood tree had been planted that day at the White House, with its spring flowers and deep, enduring roots, that a "tree takes a long time to grow, and wounds take a long time to heal. But we must begin. Those who are lost now belong to God. Someday we will be with them. But until that happens, their legacy must be our lives."

The next day, Sunday, April 23, the FBI planned to take Bill to visit Tim at the federal prison in El Reno, Oklahoma, where he was being held in custody. It was Tim's twenty-seventh birthday. It would be the first time in his life that Bill had ever visited anyone in prison.

Before they set out, the agents met Bill for breakfast at the hotel. The restaurant was full of journalists.

"No one knew who I was," Bill remembered. "We're sitting there and the waiter says, 'You guys, FBI, anyone that's got anything to do with the bombing gets a free breakfast.' A guy behind us leans over and says, 'Do writers get it too?' The waiter says, 'Hell, no!'"

"On Sunday, they had me go to Tim and ask him who was in on it with him," Bill told me. "That was the first time I got to see him. He wouldn't say nothing. Just the two of us alone in his cell. He didn't want to talk much. I was only in there fifteen, twenty minutes."

I asked Bill how he had felt. "I would say baffled is a good word," he replied.

Bill struggled to describe how his son looked at that moment. "I'd say scared. Looked different. He was probably in shock. I was definitely in shock."

Bill was only a few feet out of the cell when the lead investigator started pumping Bill for information. "I can't ask you what he said, but what did he say?" Bill remembers the man asking. Bill told the truth: his son had told him nothing.

Agents would be able to find the two men who had helped Timothy McVeigh, though, without any assistance from McVeigh. Two days earlier, the FBI had arrested Terry Nichols in Herington, Kansas, on a material witness warrant. Michael Fortier was identified later as a coconspirator. Fortier eventually struck a plea deal that resulted in only a twelve-year sentence for his role in the bombing. Nichols is doing a life sentence for his.

Bill returned home the next day, Monday, April 24. He got a call from his union rep telling him that GM management wanted Bill to take a few weeks off of work, that he should stay away from the plant. Bill stayed out less than two weeks when he asked to come in, eager to get back to work and his normal routine.

When he returned to the plant, Bill skipped his usual stop at the break room with the picnic table where workers would gather for coffee and cookies. Instead, Bill went straight to his machine without stopping to talk to anyone, unsure of how they might feel toward him. One by one, Bill's coworkers came to shake his hand and welcome him back. He learned later that one person had put a note that said "baby killer" on his locker, but that someone else had torn it off.

On the day that Bill returned from Oklahoma, the Oklahoma House of Representatives adopted a resolution thanking people who had surrounded Oklahoma City with solidarity, "ensuring this cowardly, evil attack does not achieve its goal of planting dissension and fear in the United States . . . the people of this state and nation have responded to unspeakable violence and cowardice with unsurpassed courage and compassion."

The next day, Tuesday, April 25, Bud was at Epiphany of the Lord Catholic Church on Britton Road and Rockwell in Oklahoma City for Julie's funeral. Bud's memories of that day are jumbled. "There were just so many things during that time frame I shut out," he said, but one clear memory remains.

Bud's large family of sisters and brothers gathered at his house to drive him to the service. As they started down the street, Bud suddenly told them to go back. "I forgot to get Damn Bear!" he said.

It was Bud's nickname for Julie's stuffed animal teddy bear, the one she had slept with almost every night of her life and taken with her to college. Bud ran back into his house and picked up the bear, to place with Julie in her casket.

Normally, Catholics don't open the casket at a funeral. Bud and Lena, though, told the priest they wanted it open after the Mass. Many of Julie's young friends had come in from around the country late Monday night for the Tuesday service and had not had a chance to view her body. They wanted to see her, almost as if disbelieving till they did. The priest obeyed their wishes.

The casket was decked with roses. After the service, a young woman from Chicago who had come to the funeral told Bud about a convent there. The nuns take roses and turn them into rosary beads, then make rosaries out of the beads. Bud gave her Julie's flowers, and later was given two of the rosaries made from them. "They smell just like roses," Bud said.

Bud took me to where Julie is buried, in Resurrection Memorial Cemetery in Oklahoma City, a wide, windswept place. Pine and cedar trees whose branches lean to one side flank the grave. An empty plot sits beside the one where Julie lies. Bud will be buried there next to Julie when he dies.

An anonymous man from California donated the gravesites around the time of the bombing. To this day, Bud has never learned his identity.

On the day of Julie's funeral, Oklahoma City's major newspaper, then named *The Daily Oklahoman,* ran an editorial praising the rescuers who traveled to Oklahoma City from as far as Arizona, Florida, New York, Washington state, California, Maryland, and Virginia.

"These men and women saw unspeakable horror here and found so few signs of life," the editorial stated. "But they became heroes in a city that suddenly discovered it is full of heroes . . . They moved a mountain for us. They wept with us. They experienced Oklahoma at its darkest, and yet its finest, hour."

We have ways—traditions, rituals, ceremonies—to mark the immediate aftermath of tragedy. Those days, right after a death, are a blur of mourners and services and expressions of support. But then come the days after that, when people go back to their lives and the rituals are complete. Then, with the same heavy hearts, we are alone.

Bud was left without his daughter, Julie, who now lay beneath the earth. Bill was hounded by the press as he tried to go back to work and life in his small town—now as the father of the worst domestic mass murderer in the nation's history.

CHAPTER 9

VALLEY OF THE SHADOW

In the wake of the bombing, Bud was engulfed by rage. He wanted Timothy McVeigh to die.

Bud was not alone in that. Spray-painted in blood-red paint on a brick wall near the bomb site was a message from Rescue Team 5, a unit immersed in the awful work of searching the site for victims' remains: "We search for the truth. We seek justice. The courts require it. The victims cry for it. And GOD demands it!"

Bud was drinking every night and smoking three or four packs of cigarettes a day. Nightly, he poured rum and Cokes and downed them until sleep overtook him. Daily, he woke with his head throbbing. In the afternoons, during the lunch hour before the evening rush at the gas station, he went to the site where Julie died, standing at the chain-link fence, which was decked with teddy bears and flowers left there by people who had come to mourn.

"Immediately after her death, I wanted McVeigh and Nichols dead. I didn't care with or without a trial," Bud told me. "I was just so angry and full of grief."

In the weeks and months after the bombing, Bud started having nightmares. "I kept waking up, dreaming I had been talking to Julie."

Bud's chain-smoking all day and near-blackout drinking at night weren't helping. "I was looking for something to help, and the two things I was doing were making it worse."

Bud's regular customers at the gas station noticed. One of them said to him, "Bud, you're killing yourself." Bud shot back a look of, *I don't care.* "The sooner I die, the sooner I get to be in heaven with Julie," Bud replied.

The clergy at his Catholic church didn't help either. "They tend to kind of stay away from you—just like close friends. Priests back then were trained in theology, but not in how to help people in times like that. I had some times I felt lost after Julie's death. Friends didn't know what to say to you."

Lost. Governor Frank Keating met Bud during these days and used that same word to describe him. "He was the face of anguish. He just looked lost."

On April 27, 1995, a preliminary hearing at the US District Court for the Western District of Oklahoma revealed the grand jury indictment of Timothy McVeigh and Terry Nichols on counts of conspiracy to "kill and injure innocent persons and to damage property of the

United States"; use of a weapon of mass destruction; destruction by explosive; and first-degree murder.

The indictment listed the names and ages of all of the dead, stunning in its revelation of the cruelty of the loss. Both the oldest victim, Charles Hurlburt, a seventy-three-year-old man, and the youngest, Gabreon Bruce, age three months, were visitors to the Social Security office where Julie worked.

The shattered Murrah building had to stay up because the bodies of three remaining victims were still inside: credit union employees Christy Rosas and Virginia M. Thompson, and customer Alvin J. Justes. Thompson's two sons, wearing hard hats, were allowed to go to the site and lay flowers near the place in the twisted debris where their fallen mother was thought to lie.

Once the last three bodies were recovered, authorities decided the best way to bring the rest of the structure down was implosion. Controlled Demolition, Inc., was hired to do the job. The company saved granite from undamaged portions of the building, to be used later in any future memorial for victims, but planned to blow up and remove whatever remained. A date was set for the implosion: May 24, 1995, at 7:00 a.m.

Just before the damaged building was to fall, families of victims who died in the bombing were given a chance to see up close the building where their loved ones perished. My friend Dixie Hendrix was there.

"They let family members go to the site for the first time but told all the mental health workers to come, and to wear sneakers. They wanted us to try to stop family members if they tried to fling themselves on the wreckage," Dixie told me. None did.

"I knew they wouldn't want to," Dixie said. "They just wanted to see the place where their loved ones had died."

Thunderstorms had swept through the day before, leaving behind rain-soaked streets and strong winds. Dixie wore a rain jacket. She parked her car far from the site and walked through the streets around the building for the first time since the blast. Windows from the ground to the fifth story were boarded up because the glass had been blown out.

When she got to the wrecked building, she took her place in front of it with the other mental health workers to form a human chain. Dixie stood there for eight hours as the remains of the building swayed menacingly in the heavy wind. Sheets of cloth bearing the numbers of rescue crews that workers had tied to twisted steel bars flapped loudly in the stiff gusts. The sound "only made it scarier," Dixie remembered.

"That building *moved*," Dixie told me, her voice hushed. "The wind would blow, and it would creak and moan. It was like a monster that had eaten them [the victims]." In that moment, for her, it felt as if the building itself had killed them.

On the day the building was imploded, Dixie's husband, James, made her leave town. "It felt like I was abandoning them, the families." Though Dixie still lives in Oklahoma City, she has never returned to the downtown area. She cannot bear to.

Bud was the opposite. He could not stay away. He continued to go to the site every day, obsessively.

About three months after the bombing, Bud was driving into downtown Oklahoma City for a meeting of family members of people killed in the bombing. The topic up for discussion that night was whether to erect some kind of memorial to the victims. The family group met about four blocks away from where the Murrah building had stood.

"I was going south down Robinson and saw a bulldozer doing some work on the two parking lots near the site," Bud said. "There was nothing in those lots except a tree. I knew Julie parked there under that tree. I did not want that tree bulldozed down."

When Bud got to the meeting, he sought out attorney Robert Johnson, a respected lawyer who was heading up the family group, though he had not lost a family member in the bombing. "We all had so much emotion, we needed someone to help us think straight," Bud explained.

Bud asked Johnson if he could speak to the two hundred or so family members gathered there. Johnson called on Bud to address the crowd.

"I told about the tree," Bud said. "When I went to explaining, I said, 'It is the only thing left there that survived. All of the dead have been buried. There's nothing else living except that one tree. I want that tree saved.'"

The group agreed.

The next day, when Bud was driving to his family farm in Shawnee, his cell phone rang. It was Robert Johnson. "Bob said, what tree are you talking about? I told him, it's right next to an alley, near the *Journal Record* building. I told him the tree was ugly. It leaned toward the north because of the prevailing southerly winds. It had mistletoe all through it. It shows the brilliance of Okies that our state flower is a parasite," Bud observed wryly.

Johnson said he would go and look at it. He called Bud back fifteen minutes later, and said, "You were right when you said it was ugly."

Some of the tree's branches were burned from the explosion. Its bark was pockmarked with shrapnel. Johnson got ahold of some people at Oklahoma State University's forestry department, who came down to see what the tree needed. Soon, though, care for the tree was placed in the capable hands of an urban forester, Mark Bays, who started watching over the tree like a dad watching his toddler learn to walk.

Bays grew up loving the outdoors, fishing with his grandmother and camping with his Boy Scout troop. An aptitude test he took in ninth grade cemented his choice of career: forestry. He has gone on to become the longest-serving state urban-forestry coordinator in the country. "A lot of it is spiritual," Bays told me. "I'm at peace. I go to church every Sunday, but when I go to the forest, that's my church."

Bays assembled a team of arborists from around the

nation to assess the tree. "The tree was broken, it was bent, just in bad shape. I knew it needed so much," he said. "Will it survive? It was a coin toss."

Bays told me trees are different from people; they don't heal, they seal. "When you get a cut in your hand, you put a bandaid on it and it's good as new. When a tree is wounded, it closes over. It can recover but not completely heal. Every wound that a tree gets pretty much is with it throughout its whole life."

Because Bays wasn't sure the tree would make it, the first thing he did was collect seeds from the tree, so that if it died, its offspring at least would live on. The seeds are now gathered every year and turned into saplings that are given away to the public on the anniversary of the bombing.

The second thing Bays did was free the tree from the asphalt surrounding it. When a crew showed up with massive bulldozers to do the removal, though, Bays called a halt: "I had to say, slow down, we don't know where the tree's roots are." He talked the workers into doing the job by hand. Later, Bays saw that the jackhammer operator who had carved away the asphalt had created a bed of dirt in the shape of the state of Oklahoma, with the tree nestled safely in the middle.

Bays was being inundated with well-meaning advice about how to save the tree. He responded with caution. "The fact that it had been able to survive in this lot—I feared if you give it too much, the tree might not be ready for it. You could kill it with kindness."

He and his team enriched the soil—what Bays calls "good Oklahoma red clay"—and built an underground system to bring air and water to the tree's roots. A friend inoculated the tree against the lethal Dutch elm disease.

That friend, like most everyone else, refused to accept payment for the work. "Ever since the beginning, everyone who has worked on the tree has been humbled and honored to sustain that tree's legacy. The spirit of this tree is going to outlive anybody," Bays said.

The elm is known now as the Survivor Tree; it got that name from the speech Bud made that first night about the tree being the only living thing that survived. I asked Bud why it mattered so much to save that tree. "To me, the tree is a symbol of Julie," he replied.

And so it is—not just because she had parked her 1992 red Pontiac Grand Am in its shade when she went to work each day. The tree is quirky and stubborn, gentle enough to bend and strong enough to stay standing, like Julie.

Robert Johnson sees the tree as a symbol of the "resiliency, strength, and hope of humankind. Reflective of our community's reaction to the bombing, it bent but did not break."

The tree has become the centerpiece of the Oklahoma City memorial. An image of the tree is its logo, its symbol to the public. Johnson points to the words engraved on the memorial's promontory surrounding the tree: "The spirit of this city and this nation will not be defeated. Our deeply rooted faith sustains us."

A year passed, a year in which Bud was mired in thoughts of revenge.

"About the last day of January 1996, I was standing across the street from the fence, watching these people at the site. That first year, thousands of people were visiting from all over. It was around three in the afternoon. My head was splitting because of abusing alcohol the night before.

"Standing there, I was asking myself a lot of questions. What do you do to get rid of this terrible hate? Because the alcohol wasn't helping. By this time, neither trial [of McVeigh or Nichols] had started. I had this thought: When they take Tim McVeigh out and kill him, will that be part of my healing process? I thought about that for about a month.

"Around this time, I talked to an AP reporter. When I finished speaking to him in person, and we were walking away from each other to our respective cars, he called out, 'Bud, I bet you'll be glad when they're executed.' I called back: 'No, that's not what I want.' The reporter said, 'Can I use that?' I said, 'Hell, I don't care.'"

The AP reporter did use it. Bud's quote ran all over the world.

"When you're raised on a dairy farm and pump gas all your life, you're not real media savvy. My phone started ringing off the hook," Bud recalls. "Japan, New Zealand, Tom Brokaw. From the US, people were calling to find out who this nut was from Oklahoma. I got calls from fringe groups. I started explaining. When I was for the death penalty for Tim McVeigh, I was wanting to do the same thing he had done. It just made no sense to me."

Bud told *The Washington Post* that killing Timothy McVeigh would be an act of vengeance and rage, and "that was why Julie and the other one hundred sixty-seven people were dead—because of vengeance and rage. It has to stop somewhere."

At the same time, Bill faced an avalanche of challenges: Warding off the press that dogged him. Protecting his daughter Jennifer, who was under surveillance by the FBI. Cooperating with both the FBI and the legal team for his son, Tim. Striving to maintain a normal life: work at the plant, church, bowling, American Legion, tending his garden.

Bill found himself sucked into a whole other world he had never known: the world of judges, of courthouses, of law offices and lawyers, of the rapt media coverage that chronicled every development in the case against his son.

Bill had little use for his son's court-appointed lawyer, Stephen Jones. "Jones had fifteen lawyers working for him on this case. The government paid for it. He had this whole floor of an office building just for the defense. We used to have meetings every day the two times I was there, once when the trial started, then for the death phase."

Jones frustrated Timothy McVeigh because the lawyer mounted a defense that strayed from McVeigh's own story—that he alone had planned, designed, and set off the truck bomb. Tim wanted to raise a necessity defense, that his actions were a necessary response to the threat posed by the federal government to its citizens. Instead, Jones tried to suggest that others unknown could have had a hand in the plot.

"Jones, to me, he was there for Jones," Bill said. "He wanted to be in the spotlight all the time. We'd walk from his office to the courthouse only a block away. He'd go into shops looking at all the magazines, looking for his picture."

Oklahoma was the site of the crime, but the trial took place outside of the state. Defense lawyers had argued successfully that a fair trial for Timothy McVeigh was impossible in the state of Oklahoma. The judge ordered the case moved out of Oklahoma City to Denver, Colorado.

Bill went into Lerch and Daly Clothiers on Main Street in Lockport, New York, to buy a sport coat to wear at the trial. He did not own one. The shop employee, a woman who recognized Bill from the newspapers, helped him pick out his jacket.

Timothy McVeigh was a prisoner of such high security that authorities in Denver didn't risk transporting him from custody to the federal courthouse for trial. Instead, they built a special jail cell for him in the courthouse's basement, where he was watched by US marshals.

Because there was no jail, and therefore no meal service, Timothy McVeigh's minders had to send out for food for him. Bill explained, "When it was time to eat, he got to have his choice: McDonald's, ribs. Every day, three meals, they'd go get it for him, whatever he wanted within limits of the amount he could spend. When I went to see him, he was drinking a Big Gulp."

Bill attended the trial every one of the few days he was there for jury selection, the proceedings before the trial starts when the prosecution and defense, under supervision of the judge, pick the twelve people they want to hear the case. "They [defense lawyers] wanted them to see us, I guess," Bill surmised. "My ex-wife was there too. The lawyers wanted me there, not Tim."

Jury selection began March 31, 1997. Twelve jurors and six alternates were sworn in on April 24, 1997. Opening statements began that same day, and prosecution witness testimony commenced the next. The witnesses against Timothy McVeigh included his army friend Michael Fortier, who was given a reduced sentence for his crimes fifteen days after he testified at trial.

Neither Bill nor his daughters attended the guilt and innocence phase of the trial. It is a good thing they didn't. The stories told by survivors of the bombing victims were excruciating. One distraught mother explained why she had to put her son in the day care. Another witness spoke of her dead coworker, who had been ordering flowers for her wedding. Regina Bonny, an office mate of a pregnant woman who died, Carrie Lenz, described the ultrasound pictures of the baby Lenz had happily showed her.

Timothy McVeigh was dry-eyed during the wrenching testimony, even as men and women on the jury were openly weeping when they heard it. One of Tim's lawyers, Rob Nigh, later described it as Tim "trying to maintain his composure" and asked that his client not be criticized for it. Tim told a journalist later that he was taught to believe that men don't cry.

The defense put on twenty-seven witnesses to testify on behalf of Timothy McVeigh, including his former teachers, neighbors, and army friends. McVeigh himself never took the stand.

Bud went for part of the trial, even though "everybody knew how the trial was going to come out, the question was, would he get the death penalty," Bud said. "They had a lottery thing where they would draw names and ten family members per week could go to the trial, and they would pay your expenses." Bill was not there for that part of the trial.

Bud had seen Timothy McVeigh earlier, in Oklahoma City during court proceedings over the change of venue from Oklahoma to Denver. Bud noticed a stark change in him from then to this moment, the trial.

"When I attended the change of venue, he would lean back in his chair, act kind of arrogant. I think it was nothing in the world but nerves. He was entirely different at trial, much more subdued. I think what happened is the attorneys talked to him, they probably were viewing what he was doing." One of Tim's attorneys actually sat among members of the audience in the courtroom to see the trial from the vantage point of the public.

The trial lasted twenty-three days. Closing arguments

took place on May 29, 1997. After four days of deliberations, the jury reached the expected verdict: guilty. The jury convicted Timothy McVeigh on every one of the eleven counts against him: eight counts of first-degree murder of federal law enforcement officers, one count of conspiracy to use a weapon of mass destruction, one count of use of a weapon of mass destruction, and one count of destruction by explosives.

The jurors' decision was met with emotion inside the courtroom from the fifty survivors who were present, and with cheering from the hundreds of spectators outside the courthouse in downtown Denver.

"They had worked out a signal where they could hold up a piece of paper that would indicate guilty or not," *Buffalo News* reporter Lou Michel told me. "The judge would not allow electronic media filming or recording; they had courtroom artists.

"They got the message across that he had been found guilty by placing the verdict in windows a few stories up on the glass looking out over the area where the media was corralled on the street in a cordoned-off area. It was all a race to see who would hear the verdict first."

Lou Michel was not in that race; far away, in Pendleton, the reporter was in Bill's house with Bill and his daughter Jennifer, watching the news on TV when the jury convicted Tim. "It was intense being in that house," Michel remembered. "The eyes of the country were on that courthouse and on Bill McVeigh's home. I could watch their reaction, how pensive they were.

Jennifer was smoking one cigarette after another; Bill was upset, but taking it in stride."

Two hours after the verdict, Bill and Jennifer McVeigh released a statement they had written on behalf of the McVeigh family. Lou Michel took copies and distributed them to the horde of media outside Bill's house. It read, "Even though the jury has found Tim guilty, we still love him very much and intend to stand by him no matter what happens. We would like to ask everyone to pray for Tim in this difficult time."

Michel told me that Bill had become the spokesman for the family to spare his daughters and his ex-wife from being hounded for interviews. "People knew if they came to him, he wouldn't chase them away, he wouldn't blow them off, whether it was someone local like me or someone national like Diane Sawyer," Michel said. "He treated us all with dignity. It took the pressure off all the rest of the McVeigh family. And he was Tim's father, so he could speak with authority."

The penalty phase of Tim's trial commenced on June 4, 1997, two days after the guilty verdict, and concluded on June 11. The government called thirty-eight witnesses: relatives of dead victims, injured survivors of the blast, an employee of the day care center, and rescue and medical workers.

The witnesses included the wife of forty-year-old Alan Whicher, whose children were plagued with regret over not hugging their father goodbye that morning. Gary Campbell's daughter had once showed him with pride her office in the Murrah building, the place where she died. Sgt. First Class Greg Sohn, who lost his wife, Victoria, in the bombing, told jurors, "I have my wife's coffee cup that the children bought for her that says 'No. 1 Mommy.' Inside of that is our marriage license, two rings, and a death certificate." Sohn said he sometimes took refuge in his garage to hide his grief from the five children he was now raising without their mother.

Don Browning testified about a little girl from the day care who had been outside the building when the bomb went off. The child approached a police officer handling a sniffer dog. She hugged the dog and asked it to please go inside the building and find her friends.

The Associated Press reported that Michael Lenz, whose wife, Carrie, and unborn son, Michael James Lenz III, died in the bombing, told the jury, "In one fell swoop, I went from being a husband and a daddy to realizing it was all gone. There was no one coming home, nobody's going to be in the driveway. I lost everything."

Bill was scheduled to testify for his son at this death phase of the proceedings. Tim's lawyers knew they couldn't just call him to the stand and ask him questions; the lawyers had seen how nervous Bill gets speaking in public.

"I can't stand up in front of people and speak," Bill explained. "The day we had to do it in high school, I stayed awake the whole night before. I was scared to death."

Someone suggested that they make a movie instead,

one about Tim that Bill could narrate, that could be shown to the jury.

"I spent a day with the camera guy," Bill related. "I took him all the places Tim played as a kid, worked, went to school. When I was on the stand, they showed the film, with narrating, just to show what Timmy was like when he was a kid. So I wouldn't have to. That ain't me. You should see me shaking when I was up on the stand!"

The video opened with Bill standing against a backdrop of the rural fields of Pendleton, saying, "When I grew up, it was all farms. Tim grew up, it was half-and-half." The film showed footage from some McVeigh home movies and photos, of Tim swimming with other kids in a pool, being pulled on a sled by his grandfather, laughing as he rode on the back of a small tractor in Bill's garden, playing with a toy train as a child at Christmas.

Jurors heard that Timothy McVeigh had no criminal record before the bombing, that he had received the Bronze Star for his army service in Operation Desert Storm in Kuwait and Iraq, and that he served honorably and with great distinction in the army, from May 1988 until December 1991.

The last questions Bill was asked on the stand, by defense lawyer Dick Burr, were these:

Showing a 1992 photo of Bill and Tim embracing, Burr asked, "Do you love the Tim in this picture?" Bill answered yes.

"Do you love the Tim in this courtroom?"

"Yes, I do," Bill answered.

"Do you want him to stay alive?"

"Yes, I do."

Prosecutors chose to pose no questions to Bill on cross-examination. What could they have asked this grieving father?

With that, Stephen Jones stood and said, "Defense rests."

Bill could feel the victims' families watching him and Tim's mother as they sat in court. It was almost a relief when court was adjourned for the jurors to deliberate. Two days later, Bill got a call from one of Tim's lawyers. "Dick Burr called Friday afternoon around three, 'There's a decision.' I figured the jury didn't want to stay over the weekend," Bill said.

It was Friday, the thirteenth of June. The jury of seven men and five women had reached its decision whether Tim should live.

Bill, taut with nerves, headed back to the courtroom with Mickey and their daughter Jenny. Relatives of some of the Oklahoma City victims were close by them in the crowd.

"Standing in line, this one lady came up with her hands on her hips and stared at us and said, 'You're the parents.' A friend came up and took her away. She was going to confront us," Bill remembered.

Bill and Mickey sat in the front row, with Tim's sister Jenny between them. The jurors entered one by one and took their places. Bill could feel the assembled crowd holding its breath.

Bill's eyes were fixed on the jurors as their verdict was read: death. Journalist Jo Thomas, writing for the *New York Times,* observed, "An audible gasp arose from the families of the victims in the back of the courtroom when the jury's decision was announced. One woman broke into tears, and another smiled broadly, but most of the relatives looked serious and grim."

When news of the death sentence reached Oklahoma City, bells rang out around the city. At that moment, Bud was standing with a throng of other people at the site where the Murrah building had stood. "Media had a bunch of big TV screens set up. We could watch it there when reporters announced the decision. Standing in a crowd of people, some cheers went up. I was very disappointed. That was not what I wanted," Bud remembered. "I just told the media, the day we take Timothy McVeigh from his cage and kill him, it's not going to bring any peace to anyone."

Tim's lawyers appealed, but the appellate court that heard Timothy McVeigh's direct appeal of his conviction and sentence had little use for their argument that the emotional testimony of bombing victims and their survivors had rendered the trial unfair. "The emotional impact of the testimony stemmed directly from the enormity of the crime itself," the court wrote. "Murder has foreseeable consequences. When it happens, it is always to distinct individuals . . . Just as defendants know that they are not faceless human ciphers, they know that their victims are not valueless fungibles."

Tim withdrew his appeals voluntarily. That meant he was agreeing to his execution. "The opinion I got was that he would rather die than spend the rest of his life in jail," Bill said.

Prisoners on death row who give up their appeals are called volunteers. They volunteer to die sooner rather than later. It is a choice they make for themselves, by whatever calculus might circle through the same mind that had planned a killing.

Bud and Bill, two fathers who did not know one another yet, were crushed. Bud's hope of forestalling a death sentence for his daughter's killer was gone. Bill's hope that his son's life would be spared was shattered. A stark truth confronted them both: Timothy McVeigh was destined to die.

Both men, Bud and Bill, were walking in the dark, putting one foot in front of the other, not seeing too far ahead to where that path would lead—until they were led to one woman.

PART 3 | Redemption

CHAPTER 10

THE MEETING

The story of how Bud met Bill starts with a woman who believes in miracles.

Sister Rosalind Rosolowski (known as Sister Roz) is a Catholic nun in Buffalo, New York. I met Sister Roz on a biting cold afternoon at a Buffalo hospital, where she was visiting a dying prisoner. She took time to sit and talk with me, over hot tea with milk in paper cups from the first-floor coffee shop.

She had been easy to spot in the busy lobby. Slight and smiling, wearing a blue dress and a cap over her curly brown hair, Sister Roz radiated peace and serenity even as she bustled through the crowd. She looks you square in the face and meets your eyes when she talks. She listens intently. She doesn't flinch when you tell her something hard to hear. Sister Roz is tiny, but tough.

Her day job is working with inmates at New York's notorious Attica prison. Her night job is managing a halfway house for newly released prisoners. That job is so dangerous that her coworker, Sister Karen Klimczak, a nun in her sixties, was murdered in 2006 by one of the men they were trying to help.

Bud had given no thought to Bill McVeigh, the father of his daughter's killer, until about ten days after Julie's death. "There was a sound bite on TV about how he'd be on in the next segment," Bud said. "My thought was, 'I don't wanna see this.' I just did not want to see Timothy McVeigh's father. But I stayed and watched.

"He was in front of his house. Bill was stooped over a flowerbed. The camera and the reporter were to his right. I don't remember the questions or his answers. All I remember is that on the final question, he turned and looked into the lens. I saw this large man not only physically stooped but his eyes in pain."

Bud recognized that look instantly. "It was a pain I had been feeling. I knew that someday, I would go tell that man that I knew how he felt."

For his part, Bill McVeigh had until that moment only one brief encounter with a family member of one of his son's victims. It happened the day after his son had been arrested for the massacre. The FBI had flown Bill to Oklahoma City for questioning and put him up at the Embassy Suites. "I was having a beer in the hotel bar," Bill remembered. "Two ladies came over to me. They told me they had family in the bombing. The one who raised all the hell [a pro-death-penalty victims' family member] was there, but she didn't come over. The two ladies were nice. They talked to me. I told them I was sorry."

Sister Roz didn't know Bill McVeigh, but she had found Bud Welch by chance. She had helped form a group in Buffalo in 1997 to take action against the death penalty. "We would go with signs to downtown Buffalo and pray for those about to be executed, and also for their executioners, to have a change of heart. We needed a speaker, somebody with a twist," she told me.

On the third anniversary of the Oklahoma City bombing, in April 1998, Sister Roz read a *Parade* magazine article featuring family members of some of the victims. In the center bottom of the page was Bud.

"I knew, 'He's the guy,'" Sister Roz said. She got Bud on the phone and asked him to come to New York to speak. He agreed. "In that conversation, he says, 'How far are you from Pendleton?' I knew what he was driving at. 'Do you think you could get me a meeting with Timothy McVeigh's father?'"

Bud had wanted to talk with Timothy McVeigh himself but never succeeded in getting Tim to agree to a meeting. Bud learned later that Tim was concerned that other family members of Oklahoma City bombing victims would shun Bud for such an act. Now that Tim was convicted of the crime and under a sentence of death, time for a reconciling conversation was running out. Tim's father was a welcome alternative.

Bud figured a nun was the best possible intermediary, since he imagined western New York was like Oklahoma, where the relatively few Catholics all seemed to know one another. "I asked if she by chance knew Bill

McVeigh. She said she didn't. Later, I found out about half the area was Catholic—not like being Catholic in Oklahoma City."

Sister Roz immediately started tracking down Bill McVeigh. She began by calling Good Shepherd Catholic Church in Pendleton, New York, where Bill has attended for forty years. The red brick structure is set in a wooded area. A small cemetery spreads out behind the church, the names of past parishioners etched in gray head-stones. It is a church of neighbors. The rosary group meets once a month in a different member's house to recite the rosary. "Bereavement lunch volunteers" drop off home-cooked food for folks who have had a death in their family. The "Gardeners for Jesus" get together at the church to spruce up the grounds, pulling weeds and planting flowers.

Sister Roz spoke with the church's priest, Father Belzer. The priest knew Bill McVeigh well, and not just as one of the members of his congregation. Bill came to Mass just about every weekend. He was the guy who helped run the church's adult games—Fruit Basket Wheel, Money Wheel, Big 9—keeping track of the rules and signing all the necessary papers required for gambling games. Bill was a regular volunteer at the church's annual picnic.

Another connection helped: the priest was the brother of Bill's former next-door neighbor, Liz McDermott. Liz and her husband and kids knew all the McVeigh family as friends. Her kids used to swim in the McVeighs' above-ground pool in the back yard of their former home on Meyer Road. She and the young Timothy McVeigh had worked the game booth for kids at the parish's annual summer picnic, going together to buy the candy handed out as prizes.

Sister Roz called Liz McDermott and "told her my intention." Liz went over to Bill's house and talked to Bill to see if he would agree to meet with Bud. If anyone could persuade Bill McVeigh, it would be her.

"We were electrified," Sister Roz recalled. "This sense of, this is going to happen."

Bud was driving in the sunshine on the Hefner Parkway, a roadway that curves along Oklahoma City's Lake Hefner, when Sister Roz called back. "She had all this excitement in her voice," Bud said. Bill McVeigh had agreed to meet.

It was on. The nun had arranged the time and place: Saturday morning, ten o'clock, September 5, 1998, at Bill's house.

Bud was exhilarated, but conflicted. He had a gnawing in his heart about one thing: the location. "I didn't want to meet Tim's father where Tim had once lived," Bud said.

Bill too was apprehensive. What might the parent of someone who died at his son's hands say to him? What could he say in return? "Terrible nervous. I'm a nervous person. I was nervous when you come," he told me in his plainspoken way. "I had no idea what to expect."

Forgiveness is a risky thing, like standing in the

doorway of an airplane twelve thousand feet above the earth about to jump. Beneath you is the sure solidity of the floor where you stand; before you is air and space. You step out into the void, trusting that you will glide safely to land. You stake everything on that trust.

Forgiving someone means taking this thing you held on to—your heartbreak and hurt over a wrong someone has done—and letting it go with no guarantee of how it will all turn out.

It's risky to be the one forgiven too, because you know you have done nothing to earn or deserve it. Being forgiven is something we cannot do for ourselves; it must be given, a gift we know we cannot earn and can never truly repay.

Reconciliation can be harder and riskier still, not just to let go of the past but to come together as human beings. To be in the same room and talk, equal to equal, leaving behind who owes what to whom.

My heart was hammering just before I took that step in a visiting room at Pontiac Correctional Center in upstate Illinois, meeting for the first time the man who took three family members from me: my sister, her husband, and their unborn child. My fear was like that moment of freefall, just before the tug of the parachute bears you up.

Despite their fears, the meeting between Bud and Bill was set. The two men told no one but their families. "We kept this really secret," Bud said. "We didn't want anyone to know."

The morning of their meeting was mild and sunny. Bud woke early at his hotel near the University of Buffalo campus, where he'd been interviewed at the public radio station. Sister Roz came to pick him up in a small Ford Escort, sporting her trademark twinkly smile. The plan was for her to drop him off at Bill's and for a rental car to be left for Bud to drive back to meet her after.

Bud got in the Escort, filled with jitters. He and Sister Roz peeled out quickly, heading into the country toward Bill's house in Pendleton.

Sister Roz and Bud drove eighteen miles, Sister Roz chatting happily as Bud looked around. The landscape was peaceful, but the ride was rattling. "I didn't realize anyone had built a car as small as this one," Bud says. "It seemed like we were driving really fast and sitting with my butt really close to the pavement."

Sister Roz had only landmarks to look for to find the McVeigh home—a white picket fence or a roadside sign in fading paint. That didn't slow her down. Bud saw speed limit signs of 45 mph whiz by. He asked about something outside Sister Roz's window to get her to turn her head, then stole a glance at the car's speedometer. It read 73 mph.

"We just missed Bill's house," Bud said, "so we pulled off on a dirt shoulder, the car bouncing up and down and swerving, dirt and dust flying, and made a U-turn."

Bud and Sister Roz lurched into Bill's driveway, kicking up gravel onto the grass of the front lawn. Bud escaped from the car and waved her goodbye. "I remember my knees were shaking. I'd just had the hell scared out of me."

The house is a modest, single-story structure with a one-car garage on the left and a flagpole in front, the one that Bill told me Tim himself had put into the ground. The fenced yard in back, like those of many of the homes in the neighborhood, was huge, stretching the length of a football field.

The garage door stood open, revealing Bill's Buick parked inside. Bill, who worked making radiators for General Motors for almost thirty-eight years, buys only GM cars and will drive no other kind, not even a rental. A rototiller and gardening tools lined the worn walls. Bill's brown work boots stood by the door that led to the kitchen from the garage. It smelled of motor oil and wood and earth.

Bud approached the front steps of the house, then hesitated.

I've stood on that threshold too, between fear and forgiveness. The day before I went to visit the man in prison who killed my sister, I met his father first. Nick Biro and I arranged to get together at a coffee shop a few blocks from my house on a cold March Saturday morning. A cozy fire blazed inside; the fragrance of cinnamon and dark coffee and warm bread wreathed the air. Mr. Biro wore a heavy green sweater, setting off his silver hair. The octogenarian stood to greet me when I came in; he had been waiting for me.

Part of me was afraid that he would be distant and

inscrutable, that he would be blind to the agony of my family over what his son had done, that he might even downplay his son's responsibility for the slaughter of my loved ones.

None of that happened. Instead, Mr. Biro was humble, heartfelt, and kind. He told me how sorry he was for my family's tragedy. He thanked me for being willing to visit his son. He confessed that it was hard for him to believe the son he knew had committed such a horrific act. As a mother of two sons, I could understand that; how could it be easy to see this child you love, your own, as capable of heartless murder? It is one of the hardest kinds of honesty.

I left our meeting with items he had placed in my hand as we parted: a folded-up piece of paper with typed-out directions to the prison where his son was held, and two quarters I would need to lock my belongings in a locker at the guardhouse. I left with one thing more, this thought in my heart: *Why didn't I do this sooner?* I had waited more than two decades to reconcile with this gentle, heartbroken man.

Bill McVeigh had no role whatsoever in the killing of Bud's daughter, Julie; Bill's son, Tim, did that alone. Of that, Bud was sure. He had not an ounce of blame for Bill. Bud rejected the arguments of some that Bill must be at least partly responsible for who Tim became as an adult, that Bill should have seen his son's catastrophic attack coming and done something to prevent it.

Bud knew better. He blamed the bombing on the post-traumatic stress disorder Tim experienced from what he'd witnessed in war, and on the extremist, anti-government, white supremacist views of the friends he made during that war, bombing coconspirators Terry Nichols and Michael Fortier.

But Bud was about to enter the house where Tim had slept, where the clothes he had were kept, where he would have opened the refrigerator to get a bottle of milk or sat in the living room flipping TV channels. The place was marked by the presence of a murderer under a sentence of death who was yet living. And he had lived here, in this place; he would have walked a thousand times through the front door where Bud now stood.

Bud paused a moment, instinct telling him not to ring the bell. He knocked instead. Bill, inside, scrambled to get his shoes on, then opened the door.

The two men stood face to face: Julie's father, Bud, shorter, gray-haired, and bespectacled, and Tim's father, Bill, tall, russet-haired, and lanky. Bud put out his hand and introduced himself. Bill stepped out, took it, and with characteristic bluntness told Bud that he was shy and didn't talk much. "That's not going to be a problem," Bud replied in his easy Oklahoma twang, "because I like to talk too much!" Bud wasn't just poking fun at himself; it is true. Bud can start a story that will, delightfully, wind and meander like a dirt road through the Shawnee cow pastures where he grew up.

Bud, wanting to put Bill at ease, said, "I understand you have a nice garden in your back yard."

Bill's face brightened. "Would you like to see it?"

Bud had cracked the code: If you want to get this quiet man, Bill McVeigh, to talk, ask about his garden. He can tell you the tale of each crop he plants, and when and how he does it. "In April, plant peas, corn, onions, green beans, radishes, cabbage," he explained to me on a visit. "That's about it till the middle of May. Middle of May, zucchini, yellow squash, yellow beans, cucumbers. Winter squash, peppers, tomatoes are May 30th. Every week, I plant two rows of corn, so I'll have corn six weeks in a row."

Bill buys his seeds from the same company his father did: Harris Seeds in Rochester, New York. Bill grows food and gives it away. "People want to give me money. I says, 'I do it for a hobby. It's yours.' I freeze peas and lima beans and winter squash, but everything else I give away. Neighbors, friends, relatives, and golf buddies. I take 'em in the car and say, take what you want! In a few minutes, it's gone."

The food Bill gives to others is often needed. A friend who retired from the GM plant the same time Bill did lives nearby. The man's wife worked at the jail as a cook. The couple took in their grandchildren, then great-grandchildren, because they had no place to live. "I'll bring them a bushel of potatoes," Bill told me. "Take 'em corn. I give 'em lima beans, beets, cabbage. He brings me over corned beef."

Bud and Bill walked through the garage to the back-yard garden, a span of earth half the size of a hockey rink. There, the two men, both raised on farms, were on common ground. Both knew the warm, smooth weight of a newly laid egg in your palm, the sucking sound boots make when you walk through mud to the barn, the crisp scent of fresh hay, the milky sweet taste of corn just plucked from its stalk and shucked.

They kicked around dirt clods. Bill joked about all the rocks he had dug up out of the ground. He showed Bud the strawberry patch he had just put in.

As they walked in the gentle air, Bill finally posed a question. "Bud, can you cry?"

Bud looked up at him. "Yeah, Bill, I can," Bud answered solemnly.

"For more than three years," Bill said, the breeze lifting his shock of reddish hair, "I've wanted to cry. I've had a lot to cry about. I've tried to cry. I just can't do it."

Bill invited Bud into the house. On the way in, Bill said, "Jennifer is here." It caught Bud by surprise.

Jennifer McVeigh, the younger sister of Tim McVeigh, of all his family perhaps was the closest to him. That had gotten the attention of the FBI, who dogged her for years after the bombing. She was anguished by her brother's arrest and trial, and devastated by the death sentence imposed on him the year before. Counting down the days left till that sentence would be carried out, as appeals wound their way through the courts, was torturous for her.

Bud had seen Jennifer at court hearings in Oklahoma City when Tim was seeking a change of venue from the place where the bombing had occurred, and at his trial in Denver when his lawyers succeeded in moving the case there. Bud and Jennifer had spoken only briefly.

Bud and Bill went through the back door into Bill's kitchen. A small round wood table and chairs sat in a corner by the window overlooking the back yard. On the wall above hung a clock and some pictures, including a large, formal photo of a smiling teenaged boy.

The men sat at that table and talked for hours, with Jennifer listening quietly. The two fathers found there was much more that they had in common: Both are descendants of Irish Catholics. Both men had spent their entire childhoods attending Catholic schools; neither had gone to college. Both were working men, Bud at his gas station in Oklahoma City, and Bill at the radiator plant in Lockport, New York. Both had divorced; both were the fathers of three children. The two men were born only six months apart.

"I told him about Julie," Bud told me. "He told me a little about Tim, but seemed reluctant."

Bud looked up at the photo of the smiling teenager hanging above the table where they sat. Bud was sure: it was a portrait of the young Timothy McVeigh. He wore a dress shirt and an open, easy expression. His hair was neatly combed; his eyes were bright. It is the kind of picture you find in any home where there have been children.

It made Bud think of his daughter's formal graduation portrait, the one that hangs above the desk in Bud's home office, where he spends much of his day now.

The picture shows Julie in a glow of amber light. She is wearing an off-the-shoulder dress and a single strand of pearls, with pearl earrings to match. Her long hair is a glossy chestnut, parted to the side. She is smiling a half smile; her blue eyes look off into the distance. It is the picture of her that hangs in the memorial museum in Oklahoma City, this lovely young woman at the height of her promise.

Pictures are a way to freeze people in time: the grandmother is still a baby on the beach, the long-dead ancestor stands stiffly in his suit in front of a house no longer there. But pictures of the young are something more, a person at the fulcrum of a life, about to become an adult. Here was an image of Tim on the cusp of an adulthood that would propel him to an almost unthinkable evil, looking much like any other student in a yearbook.

Bud kept glancing up at the photo of Tim until he became painfully aware of Bill and Jennifer seeing him look. They seemed to be holding their breath. "I started feeling badly about the two of them. So I said something: 'God, what a good-looking kid.'"

Bud's words hung in the air, the quiet of the kitchen broken only by the hum of a compressor running. Bill bowed his head and looked down at the table, his fingers laced. Finally, Bill looked up and said, "That's Timmy's graduation photo." A single tear rolled down his cheek as he spoke.

In that moment, spare as it was, Bud knew a searing

truth. His only daughter was gone. Bill's only son soon would be. They were both fathers mourning the loss of a child, a wound that never, ever, heals.

Bud was struck to the heart. "I saw at that kitchen table, this father could cry for his son."

Now came the outpouring, like hail from a spring-time sky. Bud no longer had to think what he should say; the words came rushing out. That Bill was not to blame for what his son had done, that Bud didn't hate either of them, that he didn't want Tim to be executed.

Bill absorbed this wordlessly, too overwhelmed to reply. Which is harder, to forgive or to be forgiven?

The two men stayed at the table and talked a few minutes more, till it was time for Bud to go. The rental car had been dropped off in front for him to drive back to Buffalo. Bud got up to leave; Bill rose too. Bud shook his outstretched hand. Jennifer, though, walked around the table and put her arms around Bud's neck and wept. Bud, the strong son of a dairy farmer, started to weep too.

"When she hugged me, we both kinda lost it," Bud told me. "I took her face in my hands and said, 'Honey, I don't want your brother to die. And I'll do everything I can to prevent it.'"

Bud would prove to be true to his word. He spoke publicly against executing Tim before he was put to death, arguing that taking a caged man out of his cage and killing him would do nothing for Bud's healing process. The day Tim was executed in Terre Haute, Indiana, Bud decried the act to reporters from around the world who had gathered there to cover the event. He gave interviews from dawn till midnight, till his voice grew hoarse.

Bud walked out the front door to his rental car and turned to look back. Bill was standing stoically; Jennifer was still crying.

Bud got in and drove away, agonized by what he had just left. Bud had not been able to save his daughter; Bill would not be able to save his son. "I sobbed all the way to Buffalo. I was crying so hard it was hard to see out the windshield. I remembered what it was like losing Julie. I thought of what was facing Bill and Jennifer. They were going to lose Tim."

He made it back to the living room of Hope House, where Sister Roz and Sister Karen were waiting for him. Bud sat down on the sofa, wrung out from his tears. "I felt this tremendous weight falling off my shoulders. I've never felt closer to God than in that moment."

Bud was the first and only bombing victim's family member ever to come to Bill's home. Bud is the only one Bill has ever kept in touch with.

Bill could tell me little of the emotional impact of this meeting, what his thoughts and feelings were. A cloud passed over his face when I asked him to describe them. "That ain't me," he said. Bill McVeigh could tell me what he did, but not what he felt. "That ain't me," he repeated.

I think I get what he meant. This man reminds me of no one so much as my grandfather Wilbur Lee Bishop, who grew up on an Illinois farm and spent forty years working at the Caterpillar plant in Peoria, Illinois. He lived in a small brick house in nearby Pekin, Illinois, a Midwest version of Lockport, New York.

My father was my grandpa's only child; my two sisters and I were his only grandchildren. My grandfather showered us with kindness. He gave us precious gifts: geodes, small gray rocks split open, with sparkling crystals inside. But he could not say these words: "I love you." When we told him, "I love you, Grandpa!" he never once said "I love you" back. Instead, he smiled and replied, "How can you love an old man?" then patted us gently on the forearm.

But we knew. We knew he loved us, as surely as we knew his pipe was in one pocket of his cardigan sweater and his tobacco pouch in the other.

Bill McVeigh is never going to give anyone a long discourse on his inner psyche. That is not how he is built.

What he can tell you, though, is how Bud rings him on the phone every so often to talk. How Bud stopped in just to see him years later on the way to speak at a local college, and waved off Bill's concern that their long talk would make Bud late for his engagement. "They'll wait for me," Bud told him. How Bud called the day a plane crashed fifteen minutes from Bill's home, killing fifty people; he was checking to be sure Bill was okay.

That is love.

Sister Roz captured the heart of their meeting this way: "Everybody had a scab on his wound. It was so fresh. Bud had already been speaking a lot about this, but for

Bill at the time, it probably felt raw. That's his son, his blood, his baby. They found that common ground of dads. That seed of friendship was planted.

"It is monumental that it happened. Bill McVeigh is such a gentle giant. Bud might have thought that he was ministering to Bill. But maybe Bill was ministering to Bud."

Sister Roz was right, of course. Bud was no longer that man standing every day at the chain-link fence surrounding the ruins of the Murrah building, his head splitting from a hard night's drinking, his eyes red from the four packs of cigarettes he had smoked the day before. He was no longer the father so consumed with grief and rage over his daughter's murder that the death penalty for her murderer was not swift enough for him, the man who had hoped that a sniper would take Tim McVeigh out from the moment he first appeared in public.

Bud had laid that burden down, the one each of us has carried at one time or another, sometimes for so long that we scarcely are aware of its weight. He had extended the hand of grace to one who should have been his enemy. That hand was taken in return.

Instead of enmity, there was peace, peace like the songs of birds soaring over the fields at twilight. He was free.

CHAPTER 11

WHAT FOLLOWS

With Tim's execution date looming, letters started flooding in from strangers and friends, telling Bill they were praying for him and his son. One night when Bill went to bingo, the parish priest surprised him with a tall stack of notes and cards from people wishing him well.

Bill occupies such a place in the hearts of the people of Pendleton, New York, that when letters came in from around the world addressed only to "Timothy McVeigh's father," with no name or street address, Bill got them. Postal workers knew where to deliver them, like the letters to Santa Claus delivered to the courthouse at the end of the classic Christmas film *Miracle on 34th Street*.

Tim instructed that he wanted to be cremated and his ashes given to Rob Nigh, the defense lawyer "next in line" after Stephen Jones, according to Bill. Nigh was the one Tim trusted to keep secret where his remains would be deposited. Tim told his father not to even ask where that would be. "Rob knows where I want 'em" is all Tim would say.

Bill's former priest told Bill he should erect a gravestone for Tim in the plot behind Good Shepherd Church. Bill said no. "I told Father Belzer, 'You don't want Tim in your cemetery. Someone's going to find that stone and tip it over.'"

It was the same when a Pendleton Veterans Association officer pulled Bill aside one night after a meeting, wanting to know if Tim's name should be included on a plaque remembering deceased veterans from the town. Bill gave a decisive answer: no.

I asked Bill if it was painful for his son's name to disappear in this way. He replied, "I didn't think Timmy should be up there. What if the wrong person seen him, and said, 'What've you got his name up there for?'"

Tim was awaiting execution at the maximum-security prison in Terre Haute, Indiana. He told his family not to come to the execution, a request they obeyed.

Bill did go to the prison to visit Tim, though, twice. On the first visit, in the fall of 2000, Bill took his two daughters so they could see their brother before he died.

"There was glass between us, and a hole in the glass. When the girls left to go to the bathroom, Tim said, 'Dad, I know you went through a lot, and I put you through a lot, but I did what I thought I had to do.' The one and only time he ever said anything about it, like an admission. 'Cause I knew it, I knew it anyhow," Bill said.

Bill Gallagher, writing for the *Niagara Falls Reporter*

shortly before Timothy McVeigh's execution, captured it this way: "A son pleased with mass murder and hell-bent to head to his execution unrepentant, and a father deeply touched by the suffering of others, who can now only pray his son will show some remorse. It doesn't make any sense."

It doesn't. The more you get to know Bill McVeigh, this humble man who, perhaps more than anyone I've ever met, lives out the commandment to love your neighbor, the less you can fathom how the nation's worst homegrown mass murderer could have come from him.

When the visit was ending, Bill's daughter Jenny was hoping to hug Tim goodbye. She knew this was her last chance; she would never see her big brother again, alive or dead. The guards gave Tim the option of embracing his family when they departed. He turned it down.

Bill and Jenny instead put their hands on the glass that had separated them from Tim during the visit. As the guards started to lead him out, Tim turned back. He returned to the glass and put his hands up to the places where the palms of his father and sister were pressed to the other side. There they stood, in a moment of parting too deep for words, hands laid against hands.

That image haunts me: the palm of your child's hand. It is a precious thing you long to keep forever, pressed into clay in some kindergarten memento or cemented in the newly laid concrete sidewalk in front of your house. Bill could only watch as his son stepped back and the imprints of his palms on the glass faded to nothing.

Tim told Bill not to come visit anymore, but Bill could not stay away; he had to see his son one last time. Bill went alone.

On April 10, 2001, their final visit, Bill and Tim talked for about two hours. Bill could tell me little of what they said. He remembers only that at the end, a guard had asked him if he wanted to hug his son. Bill knew Tim did not want to. "He knew what was coming," Bill told me. Bill said that he would just say goodbye. He went straight from his rental car to the airport, his son not in his arms but clasped closely in his heart.

Bill knew what was coming too: he would never again see his son on this earth. As a mother of sons, I can scarcely imagine that—not just to know that I would never look into my son's eyes again or hear his voice or touch him, but to know ahead of time the date, the hour, the place, and even the manner by which he would die. I look back on the death of my little sister, Nancy, and thank God I did not know that night I hugged her goodbye in a restaurant parking lot—feeling the warmth of her body, smelling the scent of her perfume—that I would never see her alive again.

After that last visit, Bill went back home to Pendleton, where his friends were focused on how they could help him get through what was to come: May 16, 2001, the day Tim was scheduled to die by lethal injection. "I had offers from two of my bingo people: 'We've got a cabin down in the Southern Tier you can stay at for the week,'" Bill said. He thanked them but declined.

Bud was checking on Bill as well, calling him on the phone a few times a week after Tim's execution date was announced. "He's going to lose his son," Bud told the *New York Times*. "And when we take Tim McVeigh out of that cage to execute him, it isn't going to bring Julie Marie back."

Just before Tim was to be executed, journalist Ed Bradley of CBS's *60 Minutes* gathered some relatives of people slain in the Oklahoma City bombing. On camera, he asked three of them a question. One of those three people was Bud.

Bradley's question was, "If you were in a room with Timothy McVeigh, what would you say to him?"

The first person, a man, said in a voice etched with anger, "I'd say, 'Tim, why don't you be a man for one time and stand up and tell me why you bombed that building.'"

The second person, a woman, said intently, "I'd get on my knees and beg him to give us the names of the other people involved in the bombing."

Bradley listened impassively to both these answers. Then he turned to Bud.

Bud said in his plainspoken Oklahoma dairy farmer twang, "What I would do is, I'd take a picture of Julie. And I would try to place a face on one of the one hundred sixty-eight that he killed. And I'd want to point out to him that he and Julie were only three-and-a-half years apart in age. And had they been raised in the same neighborhood, they might possibly have even been buddies. And my motive would be to try to put a crack in him to where he would start talking and tell us more, and I want so bad for him to ask for forgiveness before he dies."

Bradley appeared stunned by that answer, stunned that what Bud wanted was not a reason why or the names of more people to charge with the crime. What Bud wanted was for the killer of his daughter, Julie, to see her face, to recognize his common humanity with hers. Bud wanted a plea for forgiveness, one he never got to hear.

The first time I heard Bud speak about Timothy McVeigh, Bud called Tim's execution, before they ever got to meet, "a hole in my heart." I'd always thought that was because Bud never got to hear Timothy McVeigh say, "I'm sorry." Now I see the truth: it is because Bud never got to say to Tim, "I forgive you."

Bud went on in the Ed Bradley interview with this: "Tim McVeigh has been rendered harmless where he is. And I see no gain whatsoever in taking him out of that cage to kill him." It was a refrain Bud would repeat again and again in the days to come.

Back at his home in Pendleton, Bill was besieged by the press. The US Department of Justice announced that Tim's scheduled execution in May would be put off to a later date because the FBI had failed to turn over about three thousand pages of documents to defense lawyers, who needed time to review them.

"A friend said he's surprised I didn't kill some of the people who came to the door," Bill told me. "When the execution was delayed, there was a line of people at my front door. I talked to all of them. One guy was a steel worker from Niagara Falls who came down just to say he saw what I was going through, and he was sorry."

The date Timothy McVeigh was to die was reset to June 11, 2001. The location: the federal prison in Terre Haute, Indiana, where Tim was being held. It would be the first execution of a federal prisoner in the United States in four decades.

Bud went to Terre Haute that day but did not witness the execution. He did not want to. Instead, he stood outside the prison from dawn until almost midnight speaking out against the killing that was happening behind prison walls.

Bud flew to Indiana the day before with two people from the group of murder victims' families against the death penalty to which he belonged: Renny Cushing and Kate Lowenstein. The fathers of both Renny and Kate had been murdered years earlier. Renny's father, a veteran and father of seven, had been shot to death on the steps of his New Hampshire home by a disgruntled neighbor. Kate's father, a former New York congressman who had been on Richard Nixon's enemies list for his anti-war activism, was shot and killed in his law office by a mentally unstable activist.

"At that point, I was still uncomfortable saying the word murder when I thought about my dad," Kate told me. "Bud was the beginning of the most profound healing that I ever had, because of who he is. Something about Bud that was so good, so honest and real—after Julie's murder, he had started out angry, which made me feel like there's hope, that you can someday get where he is.

"And he swore," Kate added, laughing, "so you didn't feel like he was a saint."

Kate has two children, a boy and a girl. She named her son Emmett, for Bud and for Emmett Till, the fourteen-year-old African American boy kidnapped, tortured, and murdered in the Jim Crow South. Through her work, Kate had met Till's mother, Mamie Till Mobley, who had insisted on an open casket for her only child at his funeral in 1955 so the world could see the evil done to him. The resulting outrage helped spark the civil rights movement. Kate said she sees Bud and Emmett Till as very much yoked together in this naming of her son "because of how profoundly each of them impacted a movement for good in this country."

Part of Kate's job became helping to manage the deluge of media requests for interviews with Bud as the execution date grew closer. Kate was fielding an average of fifteen calls per hour, taking messages for Bud to return when he could. "Bud was just extraordinary," Kate recalled. "I remember thinking, 'I do not know how this man is holding up,' because it was overwhelming."

Bud was not the only victim's family member against the death penalty, but Kate said he became a leading voice both before and after the execution. Kate called it "a constellation of things that come together: who he is as a human, how appealing he is, what a tremendous spokesperson he is for his own truth."

Kate, Bud, and Renny landed in Indiana late and stayed up all night, since the execution was to take place early in the morning. "I remember so clearly the sun coming up," Kate said. "I remember the earth changing from dark to light slowly, and staring out the window toward where death row was and not being able to believe it was actually going to happen."

They arrived at the prison at dawn and found a scene swarming with people, including reporters from around the world. "There were close to a thousand people there," Bud said. "It looked like only about a hundred were in favor of the death penalty, with signs like, 'Fry Him' and 'Hang 'Em All.'"

Kate spent the rest of that day "watching Bud with the grace of a million heroes just soldier through that whole thing, and knowing he had done everything he could. The sun came up, and it happened. I watched him do interviews over and over again, and I thought, is there any way these reporters can understand what he is trying to say?"

When the lethal injection had taken place and Timothy McVeigh was dead, there was no official announcement to the people gathered outside the prison. Rather, Kate said, there was a ripple as the news spread from person to person.

Kate looked at Bud and saw "a shift in his bearing— when you put your whole soul into something, including the soul of your daughter whom you loved, thinking you can maybe change the inevitable, but you couldn't."

Bud talked to reporters all day long, from 6:00 a.m. until 11:00 p.m. He spoke until his voice was a ragged rasp.

"There was one woman, she was one of the witnesses to the actual execution. She came out raising both fists, cheering the execution. I just thought it was so inappropriate—cheering the death of the man she had watched die just a short time before. I don't know her, but I'm sure she regrets it now," Bud remembered.

When it was all over, Kate, Bud, and Renny drove away. "Time rolls right over these horrors and just keeps going," Kate said. "I was exhausted and drained and tuned in to trying to take care of Bud, and knowing I couldn't. It was an honor, more than anything. It would be one of the great honors of my life to get to do anything with Bud Welch."

Bill remained Tim's loving father to the last. "He's still my son," Bill told the *New York Post* shortly before the execution. "I don't understand why he did what he did, but I still love him and I will never forget him."

Back in his hometown of Pendleton, New York, a sign was posted that day at the town hall asking reporters to let the town's residents be, adding, "We grieve for the senseless murder of 168 victims. We wish we could ease the pain of those who loved them."

Bill was not present at the execution, at Tim's request. He wasn't even in Pendleton, to avoid the media he knew would come to his door. Instead, Bill spent the day at his older daughter's Florida home for his grandson's birthday party.

Journalist Lou Michel was present, though, also at Tim's request. The McVeighs trusted Michel. Bill had first met the reporter shortly after Tim's arrest, when Bill was in his back yard working in the garden. Bill had been hitting his stray golf balls out of the yard so he could mow the lawn. Michel saw him and came through a neighbor's yard to approach Bill to talk. Michel covered the story from that moment in a manner that Bill regarded as accurate and respectful.

Michel is the oldest of nine children born to a Catholic mother, the daughter of Irish immigrants, and a Protestant father. Tim chose the *Buffalo News* reporter as the only family witness to the execution. Michel is the journalist Tim spoke to at the greatest length and most revealed himself to, including his desire to die rather than serve a long prison sentence. "Tim did not want to spend the rest of his life behind bars. He called it [the death penalty] the ultimate suicide by cop," Michel said.

Michel received a letter from Tim a few weeks before his execution. In the letter, Tim was unrepentant to the last. "He said, 'I'm sorry that people had to die, but the government kills people all the time.'"

Michel told me that even the man known as the Unabomber, Ted Kaczynski, who was imprisoned for a while with McVeigh, blamed him for the indiscriminate terror of the bombing. "Ted sent him a letter critical of it. It could have been done at night; just a cleaning man could have died."

Legal team members present to witness the execution were Rob Nigh, another lawyer from Denver, and Cate McCauley, the defense investigator who gathered mitigation evidence for the death penalty phase of Timothy McVeigh's trial.

Harley Lappin, the prison warden, and the US marshal both were there, vigilant for any order to delay. The red phone in the room didn't ring. They gave the signal.

Just before the poison began pumping into McVeigh's veins, Tim looked at Michel and his other witnesses and nodded his head. Michel took it as a sign that Tim had not been mistreated in the hours leading up to the execution. "I knew Tim wanted to go. There was a lot of emotion in that room. Cate McCauley was sobbing. He saw her crying," Michel remembered.

In Tim's right eye, Michel thought he could see a tear. "He could have had his family there, but he didn't want to put them through it. I really believe he was emotionally moved by the deep concern Cate showed. He died with his eyes open, looking up right into a camera that was beaming the images to OKC."

Ten survivors of people who died in the bombing were chosen by lottery to witness the execution in person. Peggy Broxterman, then seventy years old and a retired elementary school teacher, was one of them. Her son Paul, forty-three, died in the Murrah building on what was only his third day on the job. Mrs. Broxterman told a reporter she wanted to see Timothy McVeigh gone.

Other survivors watched from Oklahoma via closed-circuit television. Kathleen Treanor, who lost her four-year-old daughter and both her in-laws in the bombing, said she regarded the execution as a triumph over evil.

Because I am a murder victims' family member, a television news show in Chicago asked me to be on that evening, to comment on the reaction of bombing victims' relatives to the death of Timothy McVeigh. I spent much of that day listening to interviews of victims' family members who had watched him die.

Reporters asked the witnesses this question: Do you feel better now that he is dead? All of them said no. They gave the same two reasons: one, McVeigh had never said he was sorry, and two, he hadn't suffered enough.

My heart broke for them. We had killed Timothy McVeigh before he had a chance to *be* sorry, before he had a chance to hear people like Bud tell him the story of his beloved daughter, lost. And how could the suffering of this one man begin to equate to the suffering of even one of the innocent children he killed in the Murrah building?

Immediately after the execution, Tim's attorney Rob Nigh released a statement, searing and eloquent, stating that it was not only Timothy McVeigh the mass murderer who had been killed that day. It was also Tim McVeigh, Bill's son, Jennifer's big brother. Nigh went on:

Of course, we can say that it was Tim himself that caused their pain.

And we would be half-right. But it would be a lie to say that we did not double their pain and that we are not responsible, because there is a reasonable way to deal with crime that doesn't involve killing another human being.

Although we might not express it in these terms because we know better, we might say that these people are simply collateral damage, but we know too well that there is no such thing as collateral damage. There are only real people with faces and names and loved ones who may never heal because of our actions, and that is true whether their grief was inflicted by Tim McVeigh or by federal law enforcement or by us collectively.

To the survivors in Oklahoma City who have had the courage to come out against capital punishment in spite of the tremendous pain that they have suffered, I say thank you. To the victims in Oklahoma City, I say that I am sorry that I could not successfully help Tim to express words of reconciliation that he did not perceive to be dishonest. I do not fault them at all for looking forward to this day or for taking some sense of relief from it. But if killing Tim McVeigh does not bring peace or closure to them, I suggest to you that it is our fault. We have told them that we would help them heal their wounds in this way.

When it was all over, Lou Michel called Bill at his daughter's Florida home to tell him his son was dead.

"Before I went to the execution, I asked Bill, 'Do you mind if I call you after it happens and speak to you about it and what your feelings are, now that your son has been executed by the US government that he had served honorably?' He said I could," Michel told me.

Michel called Bill but didn't reach him at first; Bill called Lou back on his cell phone when he was out to dinner. Lou excused himself from the restaurant when his phone rang, and the two men talked.

"He had no anger toward the government, which I thought was pretty incredible—it was his own flesh and blood here. He felt for the people of Oklahoma City as well. I started out, 'Bill, how are you doing? How are you holding up?' I told him that it had gone without a hitch, that his son went out peacefully," Michel said.

Bill flew back from Florida that same day. Walking through the airport, he could see TV screens showing reporters at the execution site and Tim's picture. "I just walked by," Bill said. "I didn't want to look."

Warden Lappin called Bill afterward to tell him that Tim had behaved in a respectable manner. The warden told Bill that Tim had met with one of the chaplains on the way to the death chamber.

"Harley said, 'When we were walking over to the building, the chaplain said, "You know, I spoke with Tim. He sought forgiveness."'" Bill has reason to believe this is true, since his son had always been willing to talk with clergy.

I asked Bill, the faithful Catholic, if he thought he would see Tim in heaven one day. Bill answered, "I hope so." He told me he prays for Tim. When I asked what he prays, Bill glanced at me with a look that said, *No*.

I apologized; it was a line I should not have crossed. Those prayers are private and precious. They are between Bill and God, the one whose son, Jesus, forgave a thief dying on a cross beside him.

A funeral home in Terre Haute cremated Tim's body. A former police investigator, an acquaintance of Tim's lawyer Rob Nigh, took the ashes to Nigh. Their whereabouts are a mystery, the location secret. The sole piece of information Nigh made public was that they would not be scattered anywhere in Oklahoma.

Bill returned to his community, his neighbors, former coworkers, fire-company and poker-night friends, church members, and bowling league teammates. They helped get him through. Bill's neighbor, Mary Lefort, who gave birth to a son on the very day of the Oklahoma City bombing, gave Bill some wind chimes to put in his back yard so he could hear gentle music when the wind blows. Bill suspects that she is the good-hearted, anonymous person who has been sponsoring an occasional Mass for the dead said for Tim at Good Shepherd Church.

Bill told me why they all stood with him throughout his ordeal. He said simply, "They know me."

A friend gave Bill a small tree in October 2001, only a few months after Tim had been executed. Bill picked a spot in the middle of his back yard and planted the tree there. He calls it "Timmy's tree."

The tree has grown to ninety feet tall. Its leaves turn scarlet in the fall. You can see it out the window when you sit at Bill's kitchen table. At certain times of day, the tree casts a shadow on the vegetable garden Bill plants just beyond it. Bill told me that a friend came by once and said, "Bill, this garden ain't getting no sun, I'd cut down that tree."

"I says, 'Do you know what that tree is?'" Bill remembered. He explained to the neighbor, who immediately said he was sorry. He did not know that, for Bill, this flourishing maple represents his son, Tim, whose life was cut short just before the tree took root in the ground.

Bud has gotten Bill through too. The two fathers met again after Tim's execution and have been in contact regularly over the years. Bud calls Bill to talk every six months or so.

Bill never calls Bud. When Bud asked why, Bill told him he felt he didn't have the right to call.

Bud often says that he considers Bill a bigger victim of the bombing than himself. It is not just that Bill has to wake up every morning living with the truth that his son killed one hundred sixty-eight innocent men, women, and children. It is also that Bill loves his son, and he cannot talk about him—*will* not—unless asked. He can't talk about his son because Bill feels he doesn't have the right.

For most of us who are parents, it's entirely different. When people ask, "How are you?" we instinctively talk about our kids. Their classes in school, their work or activities. We answer the question of how we are doing with how our children are doing, because if they are well, we are well. The retired pastor of my church, John Buchanan, quoted this saying to me once: "You are only as happy as your least happy child."

To say that Timothy McVeigh, Bill's child, was deeply unhappy seems trivial and inadequate compared with the truth. Anger lit him like a torch, with nothing that might quench the flame but destruction. No wonder Tim looked shocked when Bill first saw him under arrest for the bombing. Timothy McVeigh must have been stunned to the core of his being, not just that he had actually done it but that he had done it and found afterward that the anger, the thirst for vengeance, was still there, unassuaged. Hate is like that.

Talking about his son isn't the only thing Bill feels he has no right to do. Once, when I raised with Bill the idea of coming with me to my hometown of Oklahoma City, he instantly swatted down the idea. "I don't have a right to go there," he said in a voice that I have learned means, *Don't even try to change my mind.*

Bill McVeigh has recognized the guilt of his son but has never disowned him. No one would blame Bill if he said, "That's no child of mine!" Bill has never considered changing his name. ("It's who I am," he told me. "If people are going to get after me, let 'em get after me.") Bill has denied neither his son nor the sickening destruction he caused. Instead, Bill has acknowledged the full weight of the wrong and yet claimed Tim as his own, quietly stating that he loves Tim, still.

Frank Keating, governor of Oklahoma at the time of the Oklahoma City bombing, got Bill right, I think. Keating knew from the bombing investigation how cooperative with law enforcement Bill had been. Keating knew too, from Tim's trial and sentencing, how heartbroken and determined to try to save his son's life Bill had been. "Out of evil, good comes," Keating told me. "It's unfortunate that his story isn't more universally known. Here is a man who loved his son and his God."

Since the execution of Timothy McVeigh, the lives of these two fathers, Bud and Bill, have taken strikingly different paths.

Bud has gone on to become one of the world's most prominent voices against the death penalty. He has traveled to almost every US state and to countries around the globe—in churches and parliaments, universities and legislators' offices—speaking Julie's name. He was on the ground in each of the states that have abolished the death penalty since 1995, playing a pivotal role in convincing them to end executions. Bud has led a very public life as a member of the board of the Oklahoma City National Memorial Foundation and a founding member of a murder victims' family group that opposes the death penalty. He has given more interviews in more places than he can begin to remember.

Nancy Anthony, of the foundation that oversees a disaster relief fund for survivors of the bombing, calls Bud "unique. There were lots of survivors who were silent. Not him."

By contrast, Bill remains in the small rural town where he has lived all his days, but for his brief stint in the army. I met Bud while traveling the world; to meet Bill, I had to knock on the door of his home. He rarely speaks publicly. Talk to Bill for very long and he will tell you about the elderly friend he goes biking with or the food he is making for his poker group—small, quiet things.

This is partly because of who Bill is: he neither wants nor seeks attention. But it is also because of who his son was. Association with Tim has been hard for Bill's two surviving children, his daughters. Some of Bill's grandchildren grew up not knowing that Timothy McVeigh was their uncle. Bill wants no one, least of all those he loves, to be the object of people's anger and hatred toward his son.

The divergent path the two men have taken is powerful, poignant, and true. Bud can travel the world and talk about his child; Bill cannot. Bud can speak to foreign parliaments; Bill tills the soil in the garden behind his house and grows vegetables he gives away to neighbors and friends. Both men are spending their lives responding to loss by doing good, each in his own completely different way.

I asked Bob Johnson, the founding chair of the

Oklahoma City National Memorial and Museum, this question: What can Oklahoma City teach a world where heinous mass killings have become common? Johnson answered thoughtfully, "I would say we felt this way at the time of the bombing; we feel this way even more now. We are all very hopeful that all peoples of the world somehow can possess a resolve to prevent violence of any kind. Somehow we can be free of the hate and divisiveness. Somehow we can have the wisdom and tolerance to achieve peace on earth. That is our wish for the world."

Bud and Bill grew up in a world defined by cycles. The cows Bud milked each morning gave birth in the spring. The corn Bill plants feeds his friends and neighbors for six weeks in late summer. The Survivor Tree will shed its leaves in the Oklahoma autumn.

But violent tragedy need not be a cycle. The seeds of hope for peace and tolerance can lie in moments like the one in which a grieving man visited the home of a man about to grieve, and they quietly walked the rows of a verdant garden together.

EPILOGUE

How do we respond to evil?

If anything can be called evil, it is the murder of innocent people—like three-year-old Zackary Taylor Chavez in the day care center, or forty-four-year-old Doris "Adele" Higginbottom in the Department of Agriculture—in service of an idea.

For Timothy McVeigh, that idea was revenge.

He said so himself in a letter he wrote, calling the bombing a retaliatory strike for the violence federal agents had done in places like Waco. Timothy McVeigh meant to inflict a blow against the federal government, to rouse other Americans to action. McVeigh "wanted to cause a general uprising in America," the appellate court in his case put it starkly.

He failed utterly. His grandiose plans came to nothing. They blew away like dust in an Oklahoma sky. There was no uprising. There was only horror and grief and aching love.

In the end, the only goal Timothy McVeigh achieved was his own death. We handed him that victory. He put it succinctly in an interview he gave before his execution, which came after he voluntarily withdrew his own appeals: "'Death penalty' is . . . would you call it an oxymoron? Death is not a penalty; it's an escape. They treat me like a trophy, like they've got me, they've won? They didn't win. In the crudest terms, one hundred sixty-eight to one."

We know what that means. He killed one hundred sixty-eight people, including nineteen children. We killed one person: him. If the death penalty is meant to be an eye for an eye, by our own math, he wins. We will never be even.

His body has been cremated and his ashes scattered to the wind. In a sense, they exist nowhere. The only person who knew for certain the undisclosed location where they were dumped—his trusted lawyer Rob Nigh—is now dead, of an illness in 2017. That memory is gone.

Timothy McVeigh's life was marked by hate, but what will last of him is only love, the love Bill McVeigh has for his son. Bill wants no public remembrance of Tim. There is left almost no earthly trace of him. But Bill prays for his son, and those prayers are eternal and indestructible. Tim lives on in Bill's memories, engirded forever by a father's stubborn care. Timothy McVeigh could not kill that.

Bud's daughter, Julie, lives in that same kind of love. She has a resting place, in Resurrection Memorial Cemetery in Oklahoma City, but she has not stayed there. She has broken out, living on in the stories Bud tells all over the world about his good and feisty and beautiful daughter.

How did Bud respond to evil? By not letting evil have the last word. Julie is still speaking.

The love of these two fathers, Bud and Bill, is less like the display cases in the Oklahoma City Memorial Museum, airtight, encasing artifacts till they are buried in the dust of eternity. It is more like the elm tree Julie used to park under that Bud helped save, the vegetables Bill religiously plants each spring.

The Survivor Tree will live on long after its own death. When the tree falls, it will continue to stand in elms that have sprung from it, living monuments to that first tree's refusal to succumb to evil.

Bill's garden grows with the same bounteous hope. The first time I visited Bill McVeigh at his home, he opened a cardboard box that had arrived in the mail.

Inside were seeds. They were enveloped in small white packets with black print on the front marking their contents: corn, green beans, potatoes, cucumbers, lettuce, onions, radishes, cabbage, zucchini, peppers, squash, tomatoes, eggplant, peas.

At the kitchen table where he and Bud once sat and talked, Bill arranged the packets into neat piles, plotting the seeds he will plant in the coming spring and summer. Shoots will come up from the earth; they will grow and bear fruit.

NAMES *of Those* KILLED

Following are the names of those murdered in the Oklahoma City bombing. They dwell safely forever in the memories of those who loved them and in the arms of God.

Alfred P. Murrah Federal Building

FIRST FLOOR

Social Security Administration

Teresa Antionette Alexander, 33

Richard A. Allen, 46

Pamela Cleveland Argo, 36

Saundra G. "Sandy" Avery, 34

Calvin Battle, 62

Peola Battle, 51

Oleta C. Biddy, 54

Casandra Kay Booker, 25

Carol Louise Bowers, 53

Peachlyn Bradley, 3

Gabreon D. L. Bruce, 3 months

Katherine Louise Cregan, 60

Ashley Megan Eckles, 4

Don Fritzler, 64

Mary Anne Fritzler, 57

Laura Jane Garrison, 61

Margaret Betterton Goodson, 54

Ethel L. Griffin, 55

Cheryl E. Hammon, 44

Ronald Vernon Harding Sr., 55

Thomas Lynn Hawthorne Sr., 52

Dr. Charles E. Hurlburt, 73

Jean Nutting Hurlburt, 67

Raymond "Lee" Johnson, 59

Airman 1st Class Lakesha
Richardson Levy, 21

Aurelia Donna Luster, 43

Robert Lee Luster Jr., 45

Rev. Gilbert X. Martinez, 35

Airman 1st Class Cartney J.
McRaven, 19

Derwin W. Miller, 27

Eula Leigh Mitchell, 64

Emilio Tapia, 50

Charlotte Andrea Lewis Thomas, 43

Michael George Thompson, 47

LaRue A. Treanor, 56

Luther H. Treanor, 61

Robert N. Walker Jr., 52

Julie Marie Welch, 23

W. Stephen Williams, 42

Sharon Louise Wood-Chesnut, 47

General Services Administration

Steven Douglas Curry, 44

Michael Loudenslager, 48

SECOND FLOOR

America's Kids Child Development Center

Miss Baylee Almon, 1

Danielle Nicole Bell, 15 months

Zackary Taylor Chavez, 3

Dana LeAnne Cooper, 24

Anthony Christopher Cooper II, 2

Antonio Ansara Cooper Jr., 6 months

Aaron M. Coverdale, 5

Elijah S. Coverdale, 2

Jaci Rae Coyne, 14 months

Brenda Faye Daniels, 42

Tylor S. Eaves, 8 months
Tevin D'Aundrae Garrett, 1
Kevin "Lee" Gottshall II, 6 months
Wanda Lee Howell, 34
Blake Ryan Kennedy, 18 months

Dominique Ravae (Johnson)-
London, 2
Chase Dalton Smith, 3
Colton Wade Smith, 2
Scott D. Williams, 24

THIRD FLOOR

Defense Security Service

Harley Richard Cottingham, 46
Peter L. DeMaster, 44
Norma "Jean" Johnson, 62

Larry L. Turner, 43
Robert G. Westberry, 57

Federal Employees Credit Union

Woodrow Clifford "Woody"
Brady, 41
Kimberly Ruth Burgess, 29
Kathy A. Finley, 44
Jamie (Fialkowski) Genzer, 32
Sheila R. Gigger-Driver, 28, and
unborn baby Gregory N. Driver II
Linda Coleen Housley, 53
Robbin Ann Huff, 37, and unborn
baby Amber Denise Huff
Christi Yolanda Jenkins, 32
Alvin J. Justes, 54

Valerie Jo Koelsch, 33
Kathy Cagle Leinen, 47
Claudette (Duke) Meek, 43
Frankie Ann Merrell, 23
Jill Diane Randolph, 27
Claudine Ritter, 48
Christy Rosas, 22
Sonja Lynn Sanders, 27
Karan Howell Shepherd, 27
Victoria Jeanette Texter, 37
Virginia M. Thompson, 56
Tresia Jo "Mathes" Worton, 28

FOURTH FLOOR

US Department of Transportation/Federal Highway

Lucio Aleman Jr., 33

Mark Allen Bolte, 28

Michael Carrillo, 44

Larry James Jones, 46

James K. Martin, 34

Ronota Ann Newberry-

Woodbridge, 31

Jerry Lee Parker, 45

Michelle A. Reeder, 33

Rick L. Tomlin, 46

Johnny Allen Wade, 42

John A. Youngblood, 52

US Army Recruiting Battalion

Sgt. 1st Class Lola Bolden, 40

Karen Gist Carr, 32

Peggy Louise Holland, 37

John C. Moss III, 50

Master Sgt. Victoria "Vickey" L.

Sohn, 36

Dolores "Dee" Stratton, 51

Kayla Marie Titsworth, 3

Wanda Lee Watkins, 49

FIFTH FLOOR

US Department of Agriculture

Olen Burl Bloomer, 61

James E. Boles, 51

Dr. Margaret L. "Peggy" Clark, 42

Richard (Dick) Cummins, 55

Doris "Adele" Higginbottom, 44

Carole Sue Khalil, 50

Rheta Bender Long, 60

US Department of Housing and Urban Development

Paul Gregory Beatty Broxterman, 43

US Customs Office

Paul D. Ice, 42   *Claude Arthur Medearis, 41*

SIXTH FLOOR

US Marine Corps Recruiting

Sgt. Benjamin LaRanzo Davis, 29   *Capt. Randolph A. Guzman, 28*

SEVENTH FLOOR

US Department of Housing and Urban Development

Diane E. (Hollingsworth) Althouse, 45

Andrea Yvette Blanton, 33

Kim R. Cousins, 33

Diana Lynne Day, 38

Castine Brooks Hearn Deveroux, 49

Judy J. (Froh) Fisher, 45

Linda Louise Florence, 43

J. Colleen Guiles, 59

Thompson Eugene "Gene" Hodges Jr., 54

Ann Kreymborg, 57

Teresa L. Taylor Lauderdale, 41

Mary Leasure-Rentie, 39

James A. McCarthy II, 53

Betsy J. (Beebe) McGonnell, 47

Patricia Ann Nix, 47

Terry Smith Rees, 41

John Thomas Stewart, 51

John Karl Van Ess III, 67

Jo Ann Whittenberg, 35

APPENDIX

US Department of Housing and Urban Development

Ted L. Allen, 48

Peter R. Avillanoza, 56

David N. Burkett, 47

Donald Earl Burns Sr., 62

Kimberly Kay Clark, 39

Susan Jane Ferrell, 37

Dr. George Michael Howard, 45

Antonio "Tony" C. Reyes, 55

Lanny Lee David Scroggins, 46

Leora Lee Sells, 58

Jules A. Valdez, 51

David Jack Walker, 54

Michael D. Weaver, 45

Frances "Fran" Ann Williams, 48

Clarence Eugene Wilson Sr., 53

Drug Enforcement Administration

Shelly D. Turner Bland, 25

Carrol June "Chip" Fields, 48

Rona Linn Kuehner-Chafey, 35

Carrie Ann Lenz, 26, and unborn
baby Michael James Lenz III

Kenneth Glenn McCullough, 36

US Secret Service

Cynthia L. Brown, 26

Donald Ray Leonard, 51

Mickey B. Maroney, 50

Linda G. McKinney, 47

Kathy Lynn Seidl, 39

Alan G. Whicher, 40

Killed in Proximity to the Murrah Building

Rebecca Needham Anderson, 37

Athenian Building

JOB CORPS

Anita Christine Hightower, 27   *Kathryn Elizabeth Ridley, 24*

Oklahoma Water Resources Board Building

Robert N. Chipman, 51   *Trudy Jean Rigney, 31*

Ｙou can see the Survivor Tree, both before and after the bombing, and Mark Bays, the Oklahoma state forester who has tended the tree faithfully for decades, in a short documentary by the Oklahoma City National Memorial and Museum, available to watch at YouTube .com. (Search "The Survivor Tree" or visit: www.youtube .com/watch?v=8A-ICA3YE3I&t.)

A Casady Hymn

Music - E. Sloan   Words - H. P. Gersman

Lord in these qui – et mo – ments As we greet each new day,
Lord in those bu – sy mo – ments When we leave this al – tar,

Kneel–ing with – in this chap – el Hear us all as we pray.
When we must face life's du – ties Guide us lest we fal – ter.

Give us grace that we may find In each heart and mind,
We must have strength from your hand That this school may stand,

Pa – tience, truth and hon – or For ev–er more.
Al – ways un – der your care Grant our prayer. A–men.

ACKNOWLEDGMENTS

Deepest gratitude to Bud Welch and Bill McVeigh, to Robert Ramana, Rhonda Hefton, Melinda and Randy Compton, Chip Oppenheim, Dan Boren, Nancy Anthony, Sandy Meyers, Father H. J. Shea, Lou Michel, Dan Herbeck, Kate Lowenstein, Mark Bays, Bob and Mary Darden, Hulitt Gloer, Randall O'Brien, Mark Osler, Scott Friesen and Sara Sommervold, Clay Bennett, Dixie Hendrix, Frank Keating, Robert Johnson, Roger Paynter, Greg Daniel, Stephanie Smith, Mick Silva, Brian Phipps, Kelly Hughes, Dede McLane, Ella Strubel, Elise Magers, Tom Schemper, Lois Welch, and to Margaret Tuck and all the teachers at Casady School in Oklahoma City who made this grateful student believe she could write.